For Grade
4

Read on Target

This Book Belongs To

**Using Reading Maps to Improve
Reading Comprehension and to
Increase Critical-Thinking Skills**

Written By:
Sheila Anne Dean, M.S., CCC-SLP
Jeri Lynn Fox, M.S.
Pamela B. Meggyesy, M.A.
Pamela Marie Thompson, M.S.

Show What You Know® Publishing

Published By:
Show What You Know® Publishing
A Division of Englefield & Associates, Inc.
P.O. Box 341348
Columbus, OH 43234-1348
1-877-PASSING (727-7464)

www.showwhatyouknowpublishing.com

Printed in the United States of America
07 06   20 19 18 17 16 15 14 13 12 11 10 9 8 7 6 5 4 3 2

ISBN: 1-59230-127-4

About the Authors

Sheila Anne Dean, M.S., CCC-SLP, received a Bachelor's Degree from Ohio University and a Master's Degree from Miami University. She has worked for more than ten years in the public schools as a speech pathologist and a speech pathologist supervisor. Her role as a speech pathologist includes collaboration with teachers, parents, and other support staff while working with students individually, in small groups, and in the classroom setting. Previous presentations have included incorporating reading skills into therapy for school success, aligning instruction to meet classroom expectations, designing effective IEPs, and enhancing communication skills for at-risk and disabled children.

Jeri Lynn Fox, M.S., holds a Bachelor of Arts Degree from Bluffton College and a Master of Science Degree from the University of Dayton. A Martha Holden Jennings scholar, she has worked in public education for more than twenty-five years as a classroom teacher and school counselor. In her current role as school counselor, her responsibilities include improving student achievement, assessment coordination, and developing supportive parent/teacher partnerships and programming.

Pamela B. Meggyesy, M.A., earned a Bachelor of Science Degree in Education and a Master of Arts Degree in literature from Ohio University. Additionally, she has studied at Oxford University in Oxford, England. A thirty-year veteran classroom teacher in public schools, she has been involved with curriculum alignment and literature selection at the district and county levels. Additionally, she has chaired a district-wide writing initiative for her school system. She also has been an instructor at Wright State University.

Pamela Marie Thompson, M.S., has a Master's Degree in counseling from Wright State University and a Master's Degree in school psychology from the University of Dayton. She has taught at the college level and worked as a counselor and program director for a mental health clinic where she supervised case managers and a partial hospitalization program. She is currently employed as a school psychologist. Her background includes experience in testing, assessment, and academic intervention. She has worked in this field for eighteen years. An often sought-after speaker, she has presented numerous workshops dealing with a variety of educational topics including program evaluation, reading comprehension skill development, behavioral interventions, problem-solving skills, a concurrent session on instructional planning for the inclusive classroom at the Ohio School Psychologists Association state conference, sessions on teaching critical-thinking skills for the Association of School Administrators in Washington State, and the International Reading Association.

The authors have worked together for more than a decade in the Northridge School District in Dayton, Ohio. Their varied educational backgrounds and experiences bring a multifaceted approach to their collaborative educational projects.

Acknowledgements

Show What You Know® Publishing acknowledges the following for their efforts in making this assessment material available for Ohio students, parents, and teachers.

Cindi Englefield, President/Publisher
Eloise Boehm-Sasala, Vice President/Managing Editor
Lainie Burke Rosenthal, Project Editor/Graphic Designer
Erin McDonald, Project Editor
Rob Ciccotelli, Project Editor
Christine Filippetti, Project Editor
Jill Borish, Project Editor
Jennifer Harney, Illustrator/Cover Designer

Dedication

To our families:

David, Sarah, Marie, Elaine, and Erin, thanks for your love.
Because of you, I truly "enjoy every day." –SAD

Richard, Amy, and Anna, thank you for the joy you bring to my life. –JLF

Joe, Mark, and Lauren; I treasure each of you. –PBM

Nathan, Olivia, and Jason, thanks for your love and encouragement. –PMT

and

To our first teachers:
our parents, by birth and by marriage,
with love and appreciation:

George and Carolyn Harrington and Carl and Marianna Dean –SAD

Charles and Edith Harlow and Richard and Janice Fox –JLF

George and Connie Besuden –PBM

Joe and Emily and Harold and Marie –PMT

Table of Contents

Introduction

What is *Read on Target?*

Read on Target is a book that has 16 reading maps to help you answer tough questions related to something that you have read. *Read on Target* gives students, like you, the tools you need to answer critical-thinking skill questions. Some of these skills include the ability to analyze the story elements, to infer, to predict, and to compare and contrast. You will also need to know how to answer questions like analyze fact and opinion, explain how the author uses contents of the text to support his/her purpose of writing, critiquing, evaluating, summarizing, and determining cause and effect. These are the important thinking skills that are found in this book. Many of these skills teach you how to break down information and to show the relationships in the text. The reading maps in *Read on Target* will guide you, step by step, through the process of answering these types of questions. Each reading map is designed to help your ability to reason and to understand what you read.

Why do you need *Read on Target?*

Sometimes when teachers or parents want to check your understanding of what you have read, they will want to know if you can reason and think critically about information. If you can answer these types of questions, you can show what you've learned. Sometimes it's hard to come up with the right answer when you don't know what the question is asking or how to answer the question. *Read on Target* will help you understand how to answer these questions. This book will also help you answer tough questions found on many of your tests. By using this book, you'll be more prepared after reading to answer those questions you know your teachers or parents will ask.

Reading and understanding what you have read are two difficult tasks that you are expected to do for every subject. When you know how to read and how to understand the text, you can participate in class tasks better and answer those tough questions. You will continue to use these thinking skills as you enter the world of work.

How do you use *Read on Target?*

Read on Target will guide you through the process of answering critical-thinking questions correctly. *Read on Target* will tell you what to look for when you are reading. You will write your answers on the reading map and use your text as you need it. It also helps you practice in your class and lets you see how someone else came up with a good answer. The next time you are asked to answer a critical-thinking question, you will be more prepared and better-equipped to provide a complete, well-thought out answer.

Activity 1

Analyze Aspects of the Text by Examining Characters

I read to figure out what the characters are like. I get to know them.

Step 1

Read the story "My New Teacher."

My New Teacher

It was Tuesday morning, and it was the first day of school! Mrs. Harrington was eagerly waiting for her students. Her brown, curly hair was always pinned up behind her head. Otherwise, it would have bounced down her back and flopped over her shoulders. Her chestnut brown hair matched the color of her soothing eyes perfectly. She loved children and teaching, and it showed.

As they walked to school, Marcus and Grace talked about how excited they were to meet their new teacher. They had heard that Mrs. Harrington greeted the children with, "Good morning, friends!" They weren't sure how she would greet them today, since it was the first day.

Mrs. Harrington had a way of making every child feel at home. On this first day when the students arrived, she greeted each one with a handshake and said, "Good morning, friends! I'm Mrs. Harrington. It's my pleasure to meet you." The students told her their names and smiled back at her. They did not know where to place their belongings, so one by one she showed them. She knew they might be a little nervous, and she wanted them all to feel comfortable. After she helped them with their jackets and backpacks, she helped each child find a seat.

Marcus and Grace were given seats next to each other near the front of the room. They were even more excited now that they had met Mrs. Harrington, and both were quite curious about what the year in her classroom would be like. Marcus looked at Grace and said, "Wow! Isn't Mrs. Harrington great?"

Grace smiled back at her friend. "She sure is! I bet we get to do all kinds of neat stuff this year."

The day had started out great! Marcus and Grace knew they would enjoy being in Mrs. Harrington's class. After the children were settled in their seats, Mrs. Harrington asked for helpers to pass out supplies. She walked around the room like a mother cat looking at her new kittens. She knew each child would be able to help in a different way, and she wanted to select the best helpers. She gently tapped Grace on the shoulder. When Grace looked up, Mrs. Harrington asked Grace to go with her to the cabinets. Together, they would find the things everyone needed to begin the new school year. Mrs. Harrington also wanted Marcus to help open boxes. There were lots of jobs on the first day, and Mrs. Harrington wanted everyone to help in some way.

Mrs. Harrington told her students that she believed every student in her class was very important. She also thought learning was most enjoyable when every student joined in because each of them had ideas to share. Marcus and Grace smiled at each other. They were glad to be in her class!

Step 2

Student Tips

To analyze a character, you need to remember:

- A character can be a person, an animal, or an object.

- What the character is like, because this affects the story.

- The story could change if you change one part of a character.

Step 3

Complete the reading maps. Use the reading maps to help you think about the character.

 © 2005 Englefield & Associates, Inc.

Analyze Aspects of the Text by Examining the Characters

I read to figure out what the characters are like. I get to know them.

Map 1.1

Character's Name: _____

Describe the character.	Write a sentence from the story that tells about the character.	What does this tell you about the character?
What does the character look like?		
How does the character act?		
How does the character feel or think?		
What does the character say?		
What good or bad thing is the character doing?		
How do others react to the character?		

Map 1.2

Analyze Aspects of the Text by Examining the Characters

I read to figure out what the characters are like.
I get to know them.

Change the Character.

Change the character to **a teacher who sleeps in class**.
Tell how the story would be different.

_____

_____

_____

_____

_____

Change the Character.

Change the character to **a crying two year old**.
Tell how the story would be different.

_____

_____

_____

_____

_____

Step 4

Read the following questions and write your answers.

1. What kind of person is Mrs. Harrington? Give an example of something she said to support your answer.

_____

_____

_____

2. Mrs. Harrington thinks about how other people are feeling. Based on what you read about her, what does she do that would tell you this?

_____

_____

_____

3. What does it mean when the narrator says, "She walked around the room like a mother cat looking at her new kittens"?

_____

_____

_____

4. How could the story be different if Mrs. Harrington slept in class?

_____

_____

_____

Activity 2

Analyze Aspects of the Text by Examining Setting

I figure out how important the setting is and how the setting affects the characters and events that take place.

Step 1

Read the story "The Day at the Park."

The Day at the Park

One day last fall, my sister, Kathy, and I went to the park. We decided to go in the early evening because the weather was nice and cool. The sun was sitting lazily on the horizon, and the wind was still. "Wow! What a park!" I said to myself as we rode into the parking lot. The gravel crunched beneath the tires of our bikes. We could see the swings, the slide, and the climbing towers.

We both jumped off our bikes and ran for the swings. We liked to see who could swing the highest before jumping off. As we ran through the grass, it brushed against the bottoms of our pant legs. It had not been mowed recently. Kathy beat me to the swings. She always likes to win! The swings had plastic seats, and the chains squeaked when we moved back and forth. After the swings, we climbed the wooden tower and played "King of the Tower." Then, we slid down the slide. It was a tall, twisting, plastic-covered slide! We hooked our legs and made a train.

After we played on everything, we were tired. Kathy looked at the sky and said, "It's getting dark." The sun was dropping out of sight. The sky looked as if it had been painted with swirls of red, orange, pink, and light purple.

I said, "We better head home. Mom will be worried about us once it starts to get dark." The evening air had turned a little cooler, and dampness had settled on our bike seats. As we rode home, I thought about the great time we had playing at the park. I hoped we could go again sometime soon.

Step 2

Student Tips

To analyze the setting, you need to remember:

- What the setting looks like. Tell where the story takes place, tell when the story takes place, and tell what you hear, feel, and smell.

- The setting affects the story. If the setting is a sunny day, you might feel warm and happy. If the setting is a dark night, you might feel scared.

- The story could change if you change one part of the setting.

Step 3

Complete the reading maps. Use the reading maps to help you think about the setting.

Map 2.1

Analyze Aspects of the Text by Examining the Setting

I figure out how important the setting is and how the setting influences the characters and events that take place.

Describe the setting.	
	Write words or sentences from the text that tell about the setting.
Tell where the story takes place.	
Tell when the story takes place.	
Tell what you hear in the setting.	
Tell what you feel in the setting.	
Tell what you smell in the setting.	
Tell what you see in the setting.	

Map 2.2

Analyze Aspects of the Text by Examining the Setting

I figure out how important the setting is and how the setting influences the characters and events that take place.

Think about the setting.

How does the setting affect the characters?

_____

_____

How does the setting affect the events of the story?

_____

_____

Now, change the setting.

Change what the setting looks like to **a park with no slides, swings, or climbing towers**. Tell how the story would be different.

_____

_____

_____

Change where the setting is (where the story takes place) to **Alaska in the winter**. Tell how the story would be different.

_____

_____

_____

Step 4

Read the following questions and write your answers.

1. Describe the setting of the story.

_____

_____

_____

2. The park had swings, a slide, and a climbing tower. Explain why this setting had an effect on the story.

_____

_____

_____

3. How would the story be different if the park did not have swings, a slide, or a climbing tower?

_____

_____

_____

4. How would the story be different if it was cold and snowing?

_____

_____

_____

Activity 3

Analyze Aspects of the Text by Examining Plot
I read to figure out the chain of events; what will happen next.

Step 1

Read the story "Math Class."

Math Class

Listen to this! Have I got a story for you! Yesterday, my friend Carrie and I got in trouble with our teacher. I just cannot believe what happened. We were sitting in math class. I love math; it is my favorite class. I leaned over to help Carrie with a story problem. Story problems are really easy for me, so I thought I would help her. That started the trouble. I told her how to get the answer, and my teacher said I was cheating!

I was not cheating. The rule in our class is we can work on our homework together. It's only important that we know how to get the answer. Our teacher said, "If our friends can help us, then that's OK." However, she said that since we were working during class time, it was not homework. It was seatwork, and she considered what we were doing cheating. Then, she told us to go to the office.

The two of us walked slowly to the office. I decided I would do all the talking. I wanted to explain why we did not think we were cheating. While we waited in the office, I became more upset about the whole situation. After we told the principal the whole story, can you guess what the principal said? He told us to write an apology letter. Writing the letter was hard for us, but we sat in the library and wrote it. After we finished, we handed it to the principal. He smiled and thanked us for taking the time to write the letter. He told us it was important to follow the rule of not working on homework in class.

Finally, we went back to class. Boy, were we embarrassed! I wonder what would have happened if we had refused to write the letter. We learned one big lesson that day—we will never break the class rules again!

Step 2

Student Tips

To analyze the plot, you need to remember:

- The plot is the chain of events in the story. The plot has a beginning, a middle, and an ending. The plot has a problem and a solution.

- The plot affects the characters and events.

- When the plot changes, the story changes. What happens to the plot if you change the order of an event? What happens to the plot if you take out an event? What happens to the plot if you change the character's actions?

Step 3

Complete the reading maps. Use the reading maps to help you think about the plot.

Analyze Aspects of the Text by Examining the Plot
I read to figure out the chain of events; what will happen next.

Map 3.1

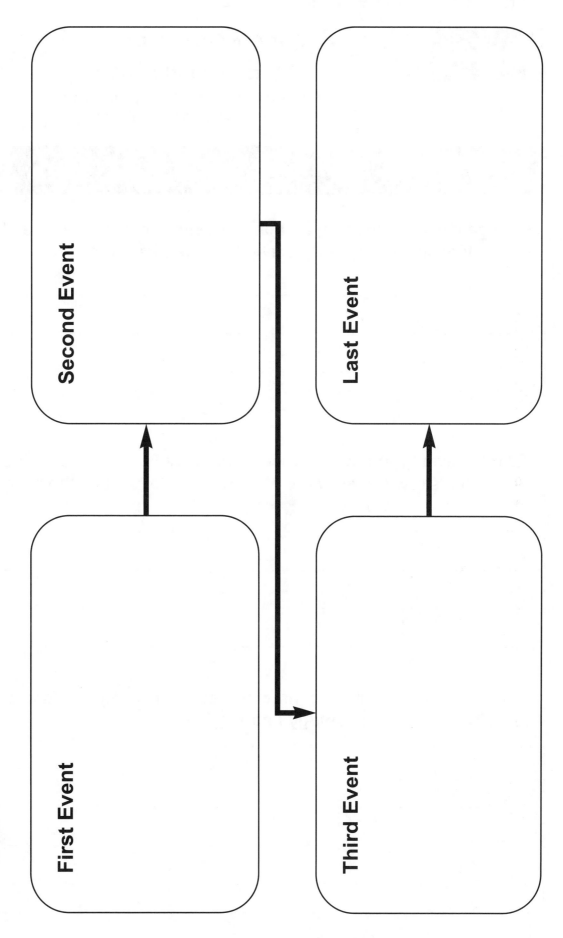

First Event

Second Event

Third Event

Last Event

Map 3.2

Analyze Aspects of the Text by Examining the Plot
I read to figure out the chain of events; what will happen next.

Change the Plot.

Change the event **(writing an apology letter)** to happen earlier. How is the story different when **this event happens earlier**?

_____

_____

_____

_____

Take the event **(girls working on homework in class)** out of the story. How is the story different when **this event is left out of the story**?

_____

_____

_____

_____

What would happen if the **characters' actions** changed to **the girls refusing to write an apology letter**?

_____

_____

_____

_____

Step 4

Read the following questions and write your answers.

1. What happens at the beginning of the story when the girls are in math class?

_____

_____

_____

2. Why did the teacher say the girls were cheating?

_____

_____

_____

3. What could have happened if the girls had completed their homework before class started? How would the story be different?

_____

_____

_____

4. How would the story be different if the girls refused to write an apology letter?

_____

_____

_____

Activity 4

Analyze Aspects of the Text by Examining the Problem/Solution

I read to figure out the problem and how it is solved.

Step 1

Read the story "Anna's Adventure."

Anna's Adventure

"Take your hat, Anna," Mother called as Anna headed for the back door.

"I've got it." Anna replied as she grabbed the red knit hat Grandma had given her for her birthday. Anna remembered how her father had laughed when she first wore the bright red hat.

"Folks will sure see you coming in that hat," he had said. But Grandma said being able to find Anna in a crowd would be a good thing, and Mother had said the hat looked fine, and besides, it would keep Anna warm.

Anna was glad to have her warm red hat. Outside, it was colder than Anna had expected. She tugged at the zipper on her jacket and pulled it up close to her chin. She then pulled the red hat down to cover her ears and forehead. The autumn air was crisp. The trees had begun to lose their leaves. In the distance, Anna could hear the sounds of tractors and combines working in the fields.

As she was walking near the creek, Anna was greeted by her dogs, Mike and Mattie. "Where have you two been?" asked Anna, laughing. Their muddy paws told her they had been in the creek. Mattie sniffed the air and rubbed against Anna's legs. This was a signal for Anna to scratch Mattie behind the ears. It was a routine Anna knew very well. Mattie wanted the attention first and then she would be on her way to explore foxholes and rabbit nests. Mike was the bigger of the two black Labrador retrievers. His chest was broad, and his face was gentle. Mike was carrying a large stick in his mouth and was wagging his tail. "Do you want to play?" Anna asked him. The big dog dropped the stick at Anna's feet. Just as Anna was about to throw the stick, Mattie's ears perked up. Then she sniffed the air. Before Anna could stop them, the dogs raced into the cornfield. "Wait for me!" cried Anna as she ran after them.

Anna guessed the dogs must be chasing a rabbit, as they were cutting back and forth through the field. Anna was still carrying the stick she was going to throw to Mike when she stopped to catch her breath. The rows where the corn had been planted were uneven and slowed Anna as she ran after her pets. At first, it was fun to run through the field. The dogs quickly ran out of sight, so Anna used her ears to follow the trail the dogs had taken. Anna's heart was pounding as she drew in deep breaths of the autumn air. Then Anna noticed how quiet it was in the field. She wondered how far she had run. That is when Anna realized she was lost. The corn was almost ready to be harvested, so it was too tall to see over, and the rows were too long for Anna to see where they led. The sun was still shining, but Anna began to feel very cold and very alone.

She called for the dogs, but they didn't come. She could not hear the dogs or any of the sounds from her farmhouse. Anna was working on a rescue plan when she thought she heard people calling her name. It sounded like Mother and Daddy. Anna tried to listen carefully, but she couldn't understand the words they were calling. She only heard the voices, and they sounded far away. Anna had an idea. She carefully bent a cornstalk towards her, then, placing her hat over the tassel tip, she released the stalk. The red hat looked like a flag waving above Anna's head. Before long, Anna could hear Daddy calling, "Anna, I'm coming." Anna wanted to run toward the voice, but he called, "Stay where you are and sing out as loudly as you can." Anna began to sing. Soon, Anna could see the cornstalks parting. She was so happy to see Daddy coming through the corn. Anna hugged Daddy as tightly as he hugged her. Daddy reached up and retrieved Anna's hat from the cornstalk. "That was good thinking, Anna. Mother saw your hat. Your hat led us right to you." Before she took her father's hand for him to lead the way home, Anna pulled on her red hat. It was good to feel safe and warm. Anna decided never to run into the cornfield again.

Step 2

Student Tips

To analyze the problem/solution, you need to remember:

- A problem from the story can be something the character wants to change or something the character wants to do.

- A solution from the story can be an action taken to solve the problem, or it can be a decision.

- The problem and solution help you understand the plot.

- If you change the problem, think about how the events from the story or the solution could change.

Step 3

Complete the reading maps. Use the reading maps to help you think about the problem/solution.

Map 4.1

Analyze Aspects of the Text by Examining the Problem/Solution

I read to figure out the problem and how it is solved.

Read the definition of a problem and a solution.

The **problem** can be:	The **solution** can be:
• A situation that the character wants to change.	• An action that helps the character understand how the problem is solved.
• Something the character wants to do or to find out.	• A decision that helps the character understand how the problem is solved.

What is the problem? _____

_____

_____

What events help solve the problem?

      Event 1. _____

      Event 2. _____

      Event 3. _____

What is the solution? _____

_____

_____

Map 4.2

Analyze Aspects of the Text by Examining the Problem/Solution
I read to figure out the problem and how it is solved.

Change the problem by making up a different problem.

The problem has changed to **Anna following the dogs to a river and getting lost**.

How would the events be different?

Event 1. _____

_____

Event 2. _____

_____

Event 3. _____

_____

How would the solution be different?

_____

_____

_____

_____

_____

_____

                 © 2005 Englefield & Associates, Inc.

Step 4

Read the following questions and write your answers.

1. What is Anna's problem?

_____

_____

_____

2. What events helped Anna solve her problem?

_____

_____

_____

3. How did Anna solve her problem?

_____

_____

_____

4. How would the solution be different if the problem changed to Anna following the dogs to a river?

_____

_____

_____

Activity 5

Analyze Aspects of the Text by Examining the Point of View

I figure out the author's choice of speaker. I also think about why the author chose to write from this point of view and how the story would be different if the story were told from another point of view.

Step 1

Read the poem "Tommy the Slowest Turtle."

Tommy the Slowest Turtle

As Tommy entered his first turtle race,
Everyone there had a very shocked face.
Tommy was tiny, so young and so slow,
The big turtles thought he would not even go.

He was the youngest reptile in the race,
Tommy the turtle walked at a slow pace.
The big faster turtles were set at the gate,
Each turtle walking his fastest of rates.

The race was so long and so tiring and hard,
The big faster turtles moved on, yard by yard.
Each one believed he was one of the best,
And figured he had enough time just to rest.

Those big, fast, old turtles, they stopped and they talked,
While Tommy the turtle continued to walk.
Surprising them all with just what he could do,
Never stopping or talking, just walking on through.

While the big turtles stopped and continued to rest,
Little Tommy the turtle just walked at his best.
Walking and walking, a very slow pace,
Not stopping or talking, he raced, and he raced.

Upon seeing the finish line drawing so near,
That tiny, young turtle soon thought he could hear,
Lots of cheering and clapping and joyful big shouts,
He knew he was winning, without any doubt!

Just then, the big turtles joined in on the fun,
They started to run, and to run, and to run.
While Tommy the turtle kept up his same pace,
That slow, tiny turtle did win the big race!

Step 2

Student Tips

- Make sure you know the definitions and key words of each point of view. You will find the definitions in the Reading Map.

- Think about the reason the author wrote from this point of view.

- Did the author write to let you know what was in the mind of several selected characters only, or did the author let you know what every character was thinking? Perhaps the author told the story to allow you to step into the shoes of the main character.

- Consider how changing the point of view will affect how you feel or think about what you have read. This will give you a clue as to why the author wrote from that point of view.

Step 3

Complete the reading maps. Use the reading maps to help you think about the point of view.

Map 5.1

Analyze Aspects of the Text by Examining the Point of View

I figure out the author's choice of speaker. I also think about why the author chose to write from this point of view and how the story would be different if the story were told from another point of view.

Point of View	Definition	Key Word Pronouns: They tell the author's choice of speaker.
First-Person	I am in the story. I tell the story.	I, me, my, we, us, our
Third-Person	Someone outside of the story tells the story from what he/she knows.	he, she, they, them
Omniscient (All-Knowing)	Someone outside of the story tells the story but knows what everyone sees, feels, and thinks.	he, she, they, them

	Write one or more sentences from the story that helped you figure out the author's point of view.
What is the Point of View? (circle who tells the story) 1.First-Person 2.Third-Person 3.Omniscient (All-Knowing)	

Map 5.2

Analyze Aspects of the Text by Examining the Point of View

I figure out the author's choice of speaker. I also think about why the author chose to write from this point of view and how the story would be different if the story were told from another point of view.

Why did the author write from this point of view?

_____

_____

_____

_____

_____

Change the point of view to first-person. How is the poem different?

_____

_____

_____

_____

_____

Step 4

Read the following questions and write your answers.

1. What is the point of view of the poem? How did you figure out the point of view of the poem?

_____

_____

_____

2. How would the poem be different if it was told in first-person point of view?

_____

_____

_____

3. Which point of view tells you how everyone thinks or feels?

_____

_____

_____

4. What point of view would an author most likely use if the poem was written as an autobiography?

_____

_____

_____

Activity 6

Analyze Aspects of the Text by Examining the Theme

I figure out the overall message the author is telling me.

Step 1

Read the story "The Gift They Gave Each Other."

The Gift They Gave Each Other

Seven-year-old George liked to play outside. He liked to run and to climb and to hide. Most days, he was covered in dirt. He also watched out for his younger sister, Stephanie. They often played in the sandbox and hid in their fort under the bushes. Their yard touched Mrs. Smith's yard on the north side and was separated from it by a row of apple trees.

Mrs. Smith watched George playing with Stephanie out in the yard and saw them building sand castles. George would help Stephanie fill the bucket and smooth the top before dumping it over. When he thought she was discouraged because the castle was crushed, he patted her back and said, "Your castle is just fine. I'll help you build the walls to make it stronger." When Stephanie got hurt, George put his arm around her to comfort her and got a bandage to make her feel better. It made Mrs. Smith feel good to see George's kindness.

George liked to play pretend musical instruments. He would use buckets for drums and sticks for trumpets. Stephanie sang along with his made-up songs. George always said, "Great job, Stephanie. I loved that song." So did Mrs. Smith! In fact, George's music brightened Mrs. Smith's days. She sat by the window just to hear their voices, laughter, and music.

Some days, George and Stephanie picked wild flowers and apples. They gathered them with care. Then, they would take their treasures to Mrs. Smith. They thought she would enjoy the treasures, but she really enjoyed the children's visits even more!

Last week, George and Stephanie saw a "For Sale" sign in Mrs. Smith's yard. When the children went inside, their mom gave them a note from Mrs. Smith. It read, "Dear George and Stephanie, I have moved to my son's house. I will greatly miss your smiles and laughter. Please continue to share your kindness with others. Love, Mrs. Smith." Mrs. Smith once said how those two children were the brightest part of her life. George and Stephanie never realized their deeds brought kindness to Mrs. Smith. They were so sad when she moved, but they knew Mrs. Smith had been a very special neighbor whom they would miss a great deal.

Step 2   Student Tips

To analyze theme, you need to remember:

- There are important ideas from the story. Look for words that tell about the story. Look for repeated words.

- The character might learn lessons. Think about how the character feels and thinks. Think about what happens to the character.

- There is an overall message of the story.

Step 3   Complete the reading map. Use the reading map to help you think about the theme.

Map 6	Analyze Aspects of the Text by Examining the Theme

I figure out the overall message that the author is telling me.

Name some of the ideas that you learned from the story.

_____

_____

_____

_____

What lessons did the character or characters learn?

_____

_____

_____

Write a sentence telling what you think the theme of the story is.

_____

_____

_____

Step 4

Read the following questions and write your answers.

1. From the idea section of the reading map, write two ideas that you learned from this story.

_____

_____

_____

2. How did the children feel after they read the letter from Mrs. Smith? Tell how you figured out the answer.

_____

_____

_____

3. What lessons did the children learn?

_____

_____

_____

4. Write a sentence explaining the theme of the story.

_____

_____

_____

Activity 7a

Infer from the Text
I read clues and use what I know to figure out what is
happening in the story.

Step 1

Read the story "Where's Charlie?"

Where's Charlie?

The bell rang for the students to come in from recess. Mr. Borger was at his
desk taking attendance. Charlie Mitchell wasn't in his seat. Mr. Borger had said
hello to Charlie earlier in the morning. He passed him coming into the building.

He asked the students where Charlie was. None of the students seemed to
know where he was. Then one student said, "He was at recess. I saw him
climbing a tree by the edge of the school yard."

Mr. Borger moved toward the intercom phone to call the office to let them
know Charlie was missing. Just then they all heard heavy footsteps running
down the hall, getting louder. Suddenly, Charlie burst into the room, his face red
and swollen. He had two big red bumps on his face. You could see a little hole in
the center of each bump. He was breathing fast, panting like a dog that was hot
on a summer day. He was swatting the air at something around him. He tried to
brush at something on the side of his head, and then it flew off.

Charlie yelled. "I was climbing a tree. I heard a buzzing, and then they were
all over the place!"

Mr. Borger picked up the intercom phone and asked for the nurse. He said,
"I think we have a problem here, Mrs. Little."

Step 2

Student Tips

To infer from the story, you need to remember:

- There are clues in the story. Clues are hints the author gives you about the story. Draw a line under each clue, or use your finger to point to the clue.

- What you know will help you figure out the story. Think about what is going on in the story. Have you done it before? Do you know about it?

- Clues, experiences, and knowledge are put together.

- Using clues from the story and what you know will help you figure out what is happening in the story. (This is called an **inference**.)

Step 3

Complete the reading map. Use the reading map to help you think about inferring.

Map 7a

Infer from the Text

I read clues and use my knowledge to figure out what is happening in the story.

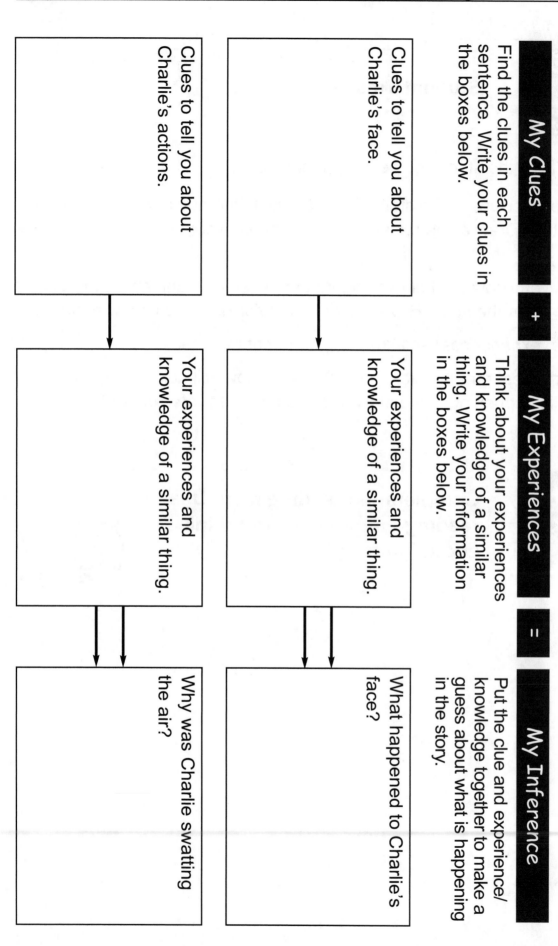

My Clues

Find the clues in each sentence. Write your clues in the boxes below.

Clues to tell you about Charlie's face.

Clues to tell you about Charlie's actions.

+

My Experiences

Think about your experiences and knowledge of a similar thing. Write your information in the boxes below.

Your experiences and knowledge of a similar thing.

Your experiences and knowledge of a similar thing.

=

My Inference

Put the clue and experience/knowledge together to make a guess about what is happening in the story.

What happened to Charlie's face?

Why was Charlie swatting the air?

Step 4

Read the following questions and write your answers.

1. What clues are there that tell what has happened to Charlie?

_____

_____

_____

2. What personal experience do you have to help you understand the clues you wrote down?

_____

_____

_____

3. What clues tell you what might have been in the tree?

_____

_____

_____

4. What might have been in the tree?

_____

_____

_____

Activity 7b

Infer from the Text

I read clues and use what I know to figure out what is happening in the story.

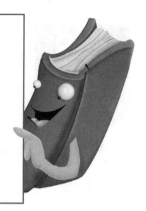

Step 1

Read the story "Animals Everywhere."

Animals Everywhere

One spring day, late in the afternoon, Elaine and Erin were walking home slowly after their long, full day. The sun had risen high in the sky. They watched it continue on its way to evening as it began to dip low toward the horizon. Their legs and feet ached, and their shoulders drooped. They had been walking around for hours and had seen many animals.

When they had first arrived, they had seen two giraffes and an elephant from a distance. The zebras were nearby, too. As the day became hotter, Elaine and Erin went inside some smaller buildings. There were bats and owls in one small building that was dark and cool inside to keep those animals and birds comfortable. The girls also enjoyed the aquarium, which was in another of the small buildings.

Then, they approached a large, outdoor area that contained another familiar animal. There were large bars and a sturdy fence to protect the visitors from him. The four-legged animal roared. He had a big, tan-colored mane. Erin read the sign in front of the fence, which said, "This animal is known as the king of the jungle." The girls were amazed to see him pacing back and forth between the rocks.

"Well, now we have seen all the animals. I sure had fun, but I am getting tired and would like to sit down," said Erin. She added, "It's getting late! We should head home."

"You're right. It's been a long day, and my feet hurt. Let's go!" said Elaine. The girls headed home to tell their families about their day.

Step 2

Student Tips

To infer from the story, you need to remember:

- There are clues in the story. Clues are hints the author gives you about the story. Draw a line under each clue, or use your finger to point to the clue.

- What you know will help you figure out the story. Think about what is going on in the story. Have you done it before? Do you know about it?

- Clues, experiences, and knowledge are put together.

- Using clues from the story and what you know will help you figure out what is happening in the story. (This is called an **inference**.)

Step 3

Complete the reading map. Use the reading map to help you think about inferring.

Map 7b

Infer from the Text

I read clues and use my knowledge to figure out what is happening in the story.

My Clues	+	My Experiences	=	My Inference

Find the clues in each sentence. Write your clues in the boxes below.

Think about your experiences and knowledge of a similar thing. Write your information in the boxes below.

Put the clue and experience/knowledge together to make a guess about what is happening in the story.

Clues to tell you where the girls are.

Your experiences and knowledge of a similar thing.

Where are the girls?

Clues to tell you what the girls saw in the large, outdoor area.

Your experiences and knowledge of a similar thing.

What did the girls see?

Step 4

Read the following questions and write your answers.

1. What clues tell you where the girls are?

_____

_____

_____

2. What experiences or knowledge do you have that helped you infer where the girls are?

_____

_____

_____

3. The text says the girls saw an animal with a tan-colored mane. What did they see? What clues were given to help you infer what they saw?

_____

_____

_____

4. What experiences or knowledge do you have that helped you infer what animal was in the large outdoor area?

_____

_____

Activity 8a

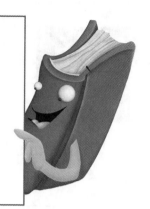

Predict from the Text

I read clues and use my knowledge to figure out what will happen in the future.

Step 1

Read the story "Flying with Monarchs."

Flying with Monarchs

In science class, Sarah and Marie learned about monarch butterflies. They studied what the monarch eats and when it migrates. Sarah loves butterflies because they have such pretty colors and fly so gracefully.

Sarah came home and told her mother all about what she learned. "Mom, did you know monarchs fly from bloom to bloom, landing gently on the petals? Butterflies have mouths that they can use like straws. They use their straw-like mouths to sip nectar from the sweet smelling blossoms. The nectar is the sweet liquid found inside. Nectar gives butterflies energy when they head south for migration."

Marie learned monarchs require warm weather to survive. They migrate south when cool weather arrives. She learned that "migrate" means they move away to find a new home in another place. Marie told her mother, "Some monarch butterflies migrate to warmer places."

To show what Sarah and Marie learned about migration, they drew arrows on the map on the next page. Look at what they learned!

When monarch butterflies migrate in the fall, they fly south toward warmer climates.

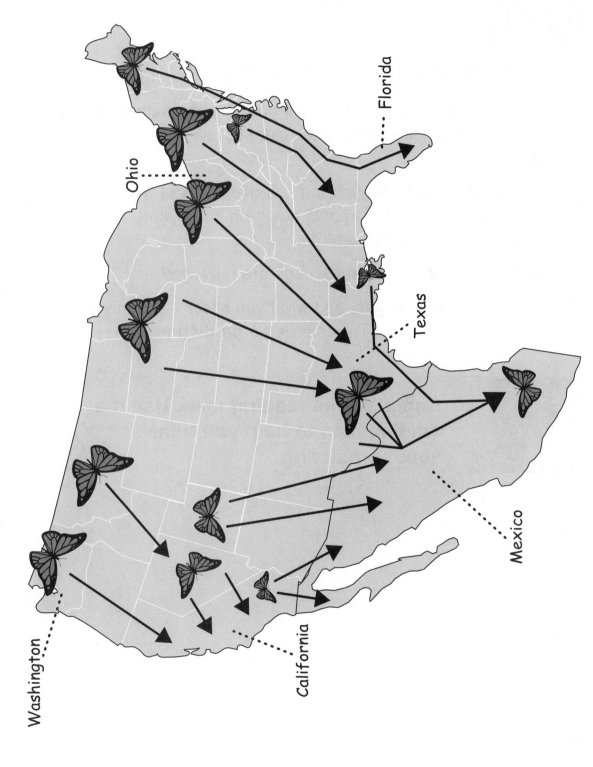

Step 2

Student Tips

To predict from the text, you need to remember:

- There are clues in the story. Clues are hints the author gives you about the story. Draw a line under each clue, or use your finger to point to the clue.

- What you know will help you make a guess about what will happen next in the story. Think about what is going on in the story. Have you done it before? Do you know about it?

- Clues, experiences, and knowledge are put together.

- Using clues from the story and what you know will help you figure out what will happen next. (This is called a **prediction**.)

Step 3

Complete the reading map. Use the reading map to help you think about predicting.

 © 2005 Englefield & Associates, Inc.

Predict from the Text

I read clues and use my knowledge to figure out what will happen next.

Map 8a

My Clues	+	My Experiences	=	My Prediction
Find clues in each sentence or paragraph that would help you answer the questions from the passage.		Think about your experiences and knowledge of a similar thing.		Put the clue and experience/knowledge together to make a guess about what will happen next.

Clues about how and what butterflies eat. → Your experiences and knowledge of a similar thing. → Do you think butterflies will eat nuts when they are flying south? Explain.

Clues about the places to which butterflies migrate. → Your experiences and knowledge of a similar thing. → Will butterflies fly long distances when it is time to migrate? Where will they fly?

Step 4

Read the following questions and write your answers.

1. Looking at the map that Sarah and Marie provided, do you think butterflies from Ohio could migrate to Texas? Explain.

   _____

   _____

   _____

2. What clues from the story helped you figure out whether butterflies could migrate to Texas?

   _____

   _____

   _____

3. Knowing that the butterfly's mouth is like a straw, predict whether or not butterflies will eat nuts when they migrate. Explain your answer.

   _____

   _____

   _____

4. Predict what will happen to butterflies living in Washington state when fall arrives. Explain your answer.

   _____

   _____

Activity 8b

Predict from the Text
I read clues and use my knowledge to figure out what will happen in the future.

Step 1

Read the story "The Secret Trip."

The Secret Trip

Carl and David are father and son. They enjoy spending time together and traveling. However, on Saturday, Carl and David are going to go on separate, secret trips. They do not want to tell anyone where they are going because they decided it would be fun to have a contest for their friends and family. The person who figures out where each one is going will get an ice cream sundae, compliments of Carl and David.

Their friends and family made predictions about the trips on notepaper at a gathering last weekend. Here is the information they received about the two trips.

Both men live in the same hometown in Washington state. David's trip is west of his hometown. When David arrives, he will see sailboats in the water. He will also see sand and seashells. David wants to buy a new sketch pad before he leaves for his trip.

Carl's trip is east of home. He will see trees, grass, and flowers high up on the land. He will drive up higher and higher, toward the sky and clouds. When he arrives, he can look down and see the small towns below. The towns look small because he is so high up. Carl will carry his favorite camera with him at all times.

When Carl and David return from their trips, they will invite their friends and family over again. Each man will tell the group where he went and what he saw. Then, David will take out the notepaper and will check to see who had the correct answers. They are certain that Marianna will have the correct answers and will win the prize, because she's been married for 40 years to her wonderful husband, Carl, and David, at 37 years old, is her oldest son. She has spent a lot of time with them and knows a lot about these two special people in her life!

Step 2 — Student Tips

To predict from the text, you need to remember:

- There are clues in the story. Clues are hints the author gives you about the story. Draw a line under each clue, or use your finger to point to the clue.

- What you know will help you make a guess about what will happen next in the story. Think about what is going on in the story. Have you done it before? Do you know about it?

- Clues, experiences, and knowledge are put together.

- Using clues from the story and what you know will help you figure out what will happen next. (This is called a **prediction**.)

Step 3 — Complete the reading map. Use the reading map to help you think about predicting.

Map 8b

Predict from the Text

I read clues and use my knowledge to figure out what will happen next.

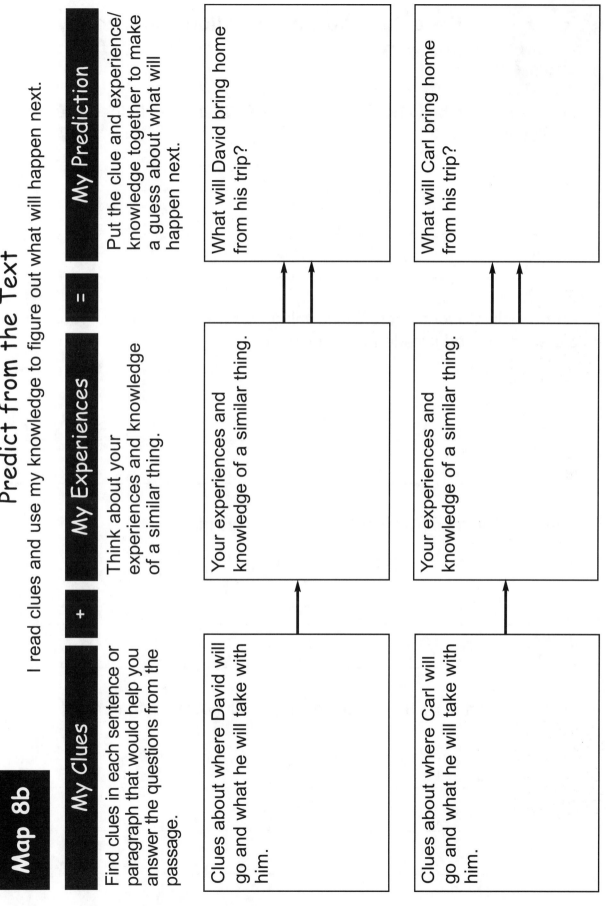

My Clues **+**

Find clues in each sentence or paragraph that would help you answer the questions from the passage.

My Experiences

Think about your experiences and knowledge of a similar thing.

= My Prediction

Put the clue and experience/knowledge together to make a guess about what will happen next.

Clues about where David will go and what he will take with him.

Your experiences and knowledge of a similar thing.

What will David bring home from his trip?

Clues about where Carl will go and what he will take with him.

Your experiences and knowledge of a similar thing.

What will Carl bring home from his trip?

Step 4   **Read the following questions and write your answers.**

1. What will David bring home from his trip? What clues helped you predict this?

    _____

    _____

    _____

2. After reading about where David will go on his trip, what are your experiences and knowledge of a similar thing?

    _____

    _____

    _____

3. Why will Carl take his favorite camera on his trip?

    _____

    _____

    _____

4. What will Carl bring home from his trip? Tell how you figured out your answer.

    _____

    _____

    _____

Activity 9a

Compare and Contrast

I read to find out how two things are alike and different.

Step 1

Read the story "Kitchens: Past and Present."

Kitchens: Past and Present

Hannah, Michael, Samantha, and Joey were helping their mother make cookies. Hannah asked, "Mommy, were kitchens always like this?"

"No, Hannah, kitchens have changed a lot through the years. For example, kitchens of the early 1900s were usually smaller, and they were very often a square shape. The floors were usually covered with a rubbery material called linoleum that you would need to wax and to buff to keep it looking nice. The stove was usually made of black iron and was heated with wood. The refrigerator, called an icebox, was much smaller than today's and was kept on the back porch rather than in the kitchen. Kitchens were much quieter without the sound of electric appliances. You would hear the sounds of the mother chopping, mixing, and stirring food by hand. The stove would have a crackling noise as a wood fire heated the food. You would also hear the splash of water as dishes were washed in the sink, and you would hear the footsteps of the iceman as he put a big block of ice into the icebox. That is why they were called iceboxes."

Joey said, "Gee, our kitchen looks much different today. It is really big and is a rectangle shape with an oval place for the table. I like our wood floor because it is easy to clean by just damp mopping instead of all that work on the linoleum floor."

The children's mother agreed. "Yes, there are lots of choices for floors today, like tile, carpet, wood, and vinyl. People today want products that are easy to take care of because they just don't have the time at home like people did long ago. We don't have to build a fire in our electric stove to get it to heat up either, and I prefer its white color to the old black iron wood stoves. Now that refrigerators don't need to have a real ice block to remain cold, they have much more room in them for food and stay much colder. I guess one bad thing about kitchens today is they are noisier. You can hardly talk over the loud motors of the electric can opener, blender, and mixer. Even the microwave oven makes a whirring noise as the food heats inside. The swish of water in the dishwasher as it washes the dishes is loud, too."

Michael replied, "What about the icemaker when it fills and drops the ice in the bin? Sometimes it startles me like somebody is dropping something in the kitchen."

"Yes, the kitchen of the past was much different than that of today," their mother said. "We still cook and eat food in the kitchen, but, oh boy, how things have changed."

Step 2

Student Tips

To compare and contrast, you need to remember:

- You are looking at what is special about each thing. Think about what makes something special, like its color and its shape.

- You are checking out how things are alike and different. **Compare** means to tell how things are alike (the same). **Contrast** means to tell how things are different (not the same).

Step 3

Complete the reading map. Use the reading map to help you think about comparing and contrasting.

Map 9a

Compare and Contrast

I read to figure out how two things are alike and different.

Directions: How would you describe the things that you are going to compare and contrast? What shape are they? What color are they? Put a plus sign (+) in a box that matches a characteristic of the other items. Put a minus sign (–) in a box that doesn't match a characteristic of the other items.

Describe the Characteristics. Tell what the things look like. Write your answer in the box next to these characteristics. (Under the shaded boxes.)	Write the names of the things that you are going to compare and contrast in the two shaded boxes below.	
Shape		+ or –
Color		+ or –
Size		+ or –
It is. . .		+ or –
Sounds like. . .		+ or –
Feels like. . .		
Write your own characteristic to compare and contrast.		+ or –

 © 2005 Englefield & Associates, Inc.

Step 4

Read the following questions and write your answers.

1. How do people cook differently today than in the past?

_____

_____

_____

2. How is the size of a kitchen different today than in the past?

_____

_____

_____

3. How are the sounds in the kitchen of the past different than in the kitchen of the present?

_____

_____

_____

4. What things do people do with their stoves that are the same today as in the past?

_____

_____

_____

Activity 9b

Compare and Contrast

I read to find out how two things are alike and different.

Read the story "Apples and Oranges."

Apples and Oranges

Mark and Lauren sat in their kitchen watching their mother dig the seeds out of an apple to prepare it for a fruit salad. Lauren thought its round shape was pretty and enjoyed looking at the different colors of apples that her mother had selected for the fruit dish. Most of all, she especially enjoyed their flavors.

Both oranges and apples were used in the fruit salad. They were the size of baseballs. Their mother had started with round oranges, which she peeled carefully and then pulled the sections apart. Then, she used large, round apples. When she cut the apples, they made a crisp, swishing sound. The oranges hardly made any noise at all.

Mark said, "Please put more oranges into the fruit salad, Mom. I love the way the orange color makes the fruit salad so beautiful. Besides, I want to use the rind for my fake smile. I like the way the rind feels so soft and bumpy at the same time."

"Why do you like oranges so much, Mark?" Lauren asked.

"Well," he answered, "let me think. I guess I like their round shape. I also like how they feel chewy when the pulp squishes in my mouth. Oranges have a taste that has a sweetness and a tartness at the same time. Sometimes, they even make my mouth pucker. And I really like the way you can smell oranges with that same sweet, citrus smell. And besides," he added, "they taste the best of all the fruit."

Lauren said, "I like apples better. They feel really smooth on the outside, and when you bite into good juicy ones, they almost squirt. Plus, they come in different colors and look really pretty in the salad. See, Mom put in yellow, red, and green ones, and they all have slightly different tastes. They can taste sweet or tart. Apples smell tart like apple cider, and I like the way they are crunchy when you bite into them. And look at the fruit salad. The pieces of red apple look the prettiest, like jewels tucked in among all the other fruits."

"Mom, which do you think is better?"

Their mom looked up and said, "Plums."

Step 2

Student Tips

To compare and contrast, you need to remember:

- You are looking at what is special about each thing. Think about what makes something special, like its color and its shape.

- You are checking out how things are alike and different. **Compare** means to tell how things are alike (the same). **Contrast** means to tell how things are different (not the same).

Step 3

Complete the reading map. Use the reading map to help you think about comparing and contrasting.

Compare and Contrast

I read to figure out how two things are alike and different.

Directions: How would you describe the things that you are going to compare and contrast? What shape are they? What color are they? Put a plus sign (+) in a box that matches a characteristic of the other items. Put a minus sign (−) in a box that doesn't match a characteristic of the other items.

Map 9b

Describe the Characteristics. Tell what the things look like. Write your answer in the box next to these characteristics. (Under the shaded boxes.)	Write the names of the things that you are going to compare and contrast in the two shaded boxes below.		
Shape			
Color		+ or −	
Size		+ or −	
It is. . .		+ or −	
Sounds like. . .		+ or −	
Feels like. . .		+ or −	
Write your own characteristic to compare and contrast.			+ or −

Step 4

Read the following questions and write your answers.

1. Compare the shape of an orange with the shape of an apple.

_____

_____

_____

2. An apple is described as "smooth on the outside," and an orange is described as "soft and bumpy." Is this a comparison or a contrast? Why?

_____

_____

_____

3. How are the sizes of an apple and an orange alike?

_____

_____

_____

4. Contrast the smell of an apple with the smell of an orange.

_____

_____

_____

 © 2005 Englefield & Associates, Inc.

Activity 10a

Analyze the Text by Examining the Use of Fact and Opinion

I figure out if the sentence can be proven or is a personal belief that tells how someone feels or thinks.

Step 1

Read the story "Caving."

Caving

My friend Amy and I were sure that caving camp would be the most exciting summer experience we could plan. The thought of crawling through caves with a few friends to see nature sounded like fun. We learned many things about this activity at our caving camp. The formal name for this activity is spelunking, and those who explore caves are called spelunkers. Most of my friends just call it caving.

Before we arrived at caving camp, we spent time gathering old clothes to wear in the caves. Old jeans, T-shirts, flannel shirts, and coveralls make great caving clothes. Dressing in layers is a must for caving. The guides at caving camp wear at least two pairs of socks, sturdy work boots, and gloves.

Our counselor told us the temperature of a cave stays the same all year. A good rule to figure out how cold it will be in the cave is to find the midpoint between the area's hottest temperature in summer and its coldest temperature in winter. Our caves are about 54 degrees all year. Once you know the cave's temperature, you can plan how many layers of clothes to wear.

At camp, we learned that wearing a hard hat is a good idea for safety. We carried flashlights, extra batteries, and bulbs. A good flashlight attached to a helmet will light the underground caverns and will allow the caver to keep both hands free for getting through the cave. When people go caving, they carry waterproof backpacks so they can carry gear and still use both hands for climbing and crawling.

The safest way to explore a cave is to travel in a team of at least four people. In case someone gets injured, one person can stay with the person who is hurt and two people can go together to get help. Before the team starts to explore a cave, they should always check in with a park ranger to let someone know they are going into the cave.

To protect the natural beauty of a cave, cavers should never leave anything in a cave. Cavers should always carry out everything they carry in. This includes their trash.

We learned that cavers get covered in mud. People should never be afraid to get dirty if they want to explore caves. They also must be willing to crawl through small openings in the rock walls in the dark. Most of all, we learned caving is a great activity for all people who like a challenge. Everyone should try caving!

Step 2

Student Tips

To analyze fact and opinion, you need to remember:

- **Facts** are true for everyone. They can be proven by seeing them or by looking them up.

- **Opinions** are true for some people. Opinions are beliefs about something. Some key words that let you know a sentence is an opinion are best, worst, bad, beautiful, ugly, always, never, everyone, mean, and kind.

- Read more about key words on the Fact and Opinion Worksheet. Then, practice writing fact sentences and opinion sentences.

Step 3

Complete the reading maps. Use the reading maps to help you think about facts and opinions.

Map 10a.1 — Analyze Aspects of the Text by Examining the Use of Fact and Opinion

I read to figure out if the reading is something that can be proven by evidence or if the reading is a personal belief that tells how someone feels or thinks about something.

Read a sentence from the story.

The guides at caving camp wear at least two pairs of socks, sturdy work boots, and gloves.

If you think the sentence is a FACT, then:	**O R**	If you think the sentence is an OPINION, then:
Write how the information that you read can be proven by evidence or observation. _____ _____ _____ Write where you would check by looking up the information or where you would see it. _____ _____ _____ Is the information true for everyone? _____		Write the KEY WORDS, which are clues that tell you how someone thinks, feels, or overstates. _____ _____ _____ Write how the information tells a personal belief or judgment about something. _____ _____ _____ Is the information true for some people? _____

Map 10a.2 — Analyze Aspects of the Text by Examining the Use of Fact and Opinion

I read to figure out if the reading is something that can be proven by evidence or if the reading is a personal belief that tells how someone feels or thinks about something.

Read a sentence from the story.

**People should never be afraid to get dirty
if they want to explore caves.**

OR

If you think the sentence is a FACT, then:	If you think the sentence is an OPINION, then:
Write how the information that you read can be proven by evidence or observation.	Write the KEY WORDS, which are clues that tell you how someone thinks, feels, or overstates.
_____ _____ _____	_____ _____ _____
Write where you would check by looking up the information or where you would see it.	Write how the information tells a personal belief or judgment about something.
_____ _____ _____	_____ _____ _____
Is the information true for everyone?	Is the information true for some people?
_____	_____

Map 10a.3 Fact and Opinion Worksheet

Facts	Opinions
• true for everyone • can be proven and supported by evidence and observation • can be checked by looking up the information or seeing it	• true for some people • tells how someone thinks or feels about something • personal belief or judgment about something

You can use key words to change a fact into an opinion. Here are some examples of key words that will help you figure out if the information is an opinion.

KEY WORDS that describe an opinion:
best, great, easy, hard, beautiful, pretty, good, bad, difficult, ugly, terrible, excellent

KEY WORDS that overstate an opinion:
always, never, all, everyone

FACT + KEY WORD = OPINION

Here is an example: 1. This is a book. (fact) 2. This is a great book. (opinion)

Practice changing a fact into an opinion.

Read a fact sentence: **Guides at caving camp wear at least two pairs of socks, sturdy work boots, and gloves.**

Add a KEY WORD to change the fact into an opinion: _____

_____

Practice changing an opinion into a fact.

Read an opinion sentence: **People should never be afraid to get dirty if they want to explore caves.**

Take the KEY WORD out of the opinion sentence and write a fact sentence:

_____

**Read the following questions and write your
answers.**

1. To protect the natural beauty of a cave, cavers should never leave
   anything in the cave. Is this a fact or an opinion? Explain your answer.

   _____

   _____

   _____

2. The cavers were covered in mud. Is this a fact or an opinion? Explain
   your answer.

   _____

   _____

   _____

3. Write one factual sentence from the story that describes what the
   guides at caving camp wear.

   _____

   _____

   _____

4. Write an opinion sentence from the story. Explain why this is an
   opinion.

   _____

   _____

   _____

Activity 10b

Analyze the Text by Examining the Use of Fact and Opinion

I figure out if the sentence can be proven or is a personal belief that tells how someone feels or thinks.

Step 1

Read the story "The Weather Chart."

The Weather Chart

The weather certainly determines where children can play. For instance, Mike, Sue, and Sam are cousins who like to play together. Since it is July, they play outside. They are allowed to ride their bikes to the swimming pool. They enjoy playing tag with their friends in the neighborhood and selling lemonade to people who walk by. Sometimes, they get out their chalk to draw animals, to trace their bodies, and to draw hopscotch boards on the sidewalk. They think there's so much more to do outside than inside.

When they play inside, they have to stay quiet and calm. They try to stay "as cool as cucumbers." It is easy for the children to stay quiet. They play games like cards and checkers. They sometimes play school. If they know they'll be inside for a long time, they start a hard puzzle. Sometimes, they make crazy creations with clay.

Some days, the children can choose where they want to play, but on other days, the weather makes it hard to plan whether they'll play inside or outside. On Monday, Mike, Sue, and Sam weren't sure about the weather. They decided to check the newspaper to see what the weather would be like for the next few days so they could plan where they would play. Sue looked in the paper for a weather chart. "Weather charts always give you correct information," she said. She found a chart called "An Easy-to-Use Weather Chart."

After looking at the chart, Mike planned to set up his indoor games Tuesday night. The chart said it would rain on Wednesday. He said, "The weather chart is easy for everyone to use. This chart is a good way to plan your day."

An Easy-to-Use Weather Chart

Today/Monday	Tuesday	Wednesday	Thursday	Friday

Partly sunny	Sunny and hot	Rain showers	Cloudy	Sunny and warm

---

Step 2 — Student Tips

To analyze fact and opinion, you need to remember:

- **Facts** are true for everyone. They can be proven by seeing them or by looking them up.

- **Opinions** are true for some people. Opinions are beliefs about something. Some key words that let you know a sentence is an opinion are best, worst, bad, beautiful, ugly, always, never, everyone, mean, and kind.

- Read more about key words on the Fact and Opinion Worksheet. Then, practice writing fact sentences and opinion sentences.

Step 3 — Complete the reading maps. Use the reading maps to help you think about facts and opinions.

Map 10b.1

Analyze Aspects of the Text by Examining the Use of Fact and Opinion

I read to figure out if the reading is something that can be proven by evidence or if the reading is a personal belief that tells how someone feels or thinks about something.

Read a sentence from the story.

They play games like cards and checkers.

| If you think the sentence is a FACT, then: | **O R** | If you think the sentence is an OPINION, then: |

Write how the information that you read can be proven by evidence or observation.	Write the KEY WORDS, which are clues that tell you how someone thinks, feels, or overstates.
_____ _____ _____	_____ _____ _____
Write where you would check by looking up the information or where you would see it.	Write how the information tells a personal belief or judgment about something.
_____ _____ _____	_____ _____ _____
Is the information true for everyone?	Is the information true for some people?
_____	_____

Map 10b.2

Analyze Aspects of the Text by Examining the Use of Fact and Opinion

I read to figure out if the reading is something that can be proven by evidence or if the reading is a personal belief that tells how someone feels or thinks about something.

Read a sentence from the story.

This chart is a good way to plan your day.

If you think the sentence is a FACT, then:	**O R**	If you think the sentence is an OPINION, then:

Write how the information that you read can be proven by evidence or observation.	Write the KEY WORDS, which are clues that tell you how someone thinks, feels, or overstates.
_____ _____ _____	_____ _____ _____
Write where you would check by looking up the information or where you would see it.	Write how the information tells a personal belief or judgment about something.
_____ _____ _____	_____ _____ _____
Is the information true for everyone?	Is the information true for some people?
_____	_____

Map 10b.3   Fact and Opinion Worksheet

Facts	Opinions
• true for everyone • can be proven and supported by evidence and observation • can be checked by looking up the information or seeing it	• true for some people • tells how someone thinks or feels about something • personal belief or judgment about something

You can use key words to change a fact into an opinion. Here are some examples of key words that will help you figure out if the information is an opinion.

KEY WORDS that describe an opinion:
best, great, easy, hard, beautiful, pretty, good, bad, difficult, ugly, terrible, excellent

KEY WORDS that overstate an opinion:
always, never, all, everyone

FACT + KEY WORD = OPINION

Here is an example: 1. This is a book. (fact) 2. This is a great book. (opinion)

Practice changing a fact into an opinion.

Read a fact sentence: **They play games like cards and checkers.**

Add a KEY WORD to change the fact into an opinion: _____

_____

Practice changing an opinion into a fact.

Read an opinion sentence: **This chart is a good way to plan your day.**

Take the KEY WORD out of the opinion sentence and write a fact sentence:

_____

Step 4

Read the following questions and write your answers.

1. Write two opinions from the text.

_____

_____

_____

2. The chart said it would rain on Wednesday. Is this statement a fact or an opinion? Explain your answer.

_____

_____

_____

3. The weather chart is easy for everyone to use. This chart is a good way to plan everyone's day. Are these sentences facts or opinions? Explain your answer.

_____

_____

_____

4. Write two facts from the story that tell you what the children might do on Wednesday if it rains.

_____

_____

_____

Activity 11a

Explain How and Why an Author Uses Contents of a Text to Support His/Her Purpose for Writing

I tell the process (how) and the reason (why) the story was written.

Step 1

Read the story "Expect Something Good to Happen."

Expect Something Good to Happen

Mario sighed and stared out the window. Since the doctor had set his cast, his arm ached only a little, but that fractured arm sure was hurting the plans Mario had made for the summer. Six weeks with no swimming, no baseball, and no summer camp would be a real pain. By the time his arm healed, summer would be almost over. Mario sighed again. It had been an awful day.

"I'm going for a walk," announced Lionel. "Want to come along?" Mario knew his older brother was trying to cheer him up, but Mario was too sad to be cheered up. He was sure his summer was ruined. "What's the point?" Mario replied. Lionel understood how disappointed Mario was feeling. He said, "Well, there just might be a bright side to your situation if you would be open to new possibilities."

Mario had heard his parents and grandparents say the same thing many times. Looking for something good to come from a difficult or disappointing situation was a family motto. Mario could not imagine how anything good could come from his broken arm, but he decided to go with his brother anyway.

The boys were barely at the end of their driveway when they saw their neighbor, Mr. Nathan. Mr. Nathan was a nice man who usually walked his dog, Zoey, early in the morning. He was walking a new dog this evening. "Nice dog, Mr. Nathan. But where is Zoey?" asked Lionel.

"Zoey is at home, resting. I found this young pup wandering near the highway. She seemed lost and hungry," said the kind man. He went on to tell the boys how he had checked the animal shelter and had placed an ad in the

---

newspaper. No one seemed to know where the spotted dog belonged. "It's too bad. This dog needs a good home. But I only have enough time to care for one dog," Mr. Nathan continued. "This is a really nice dog. She is smart, too. She knows several tricks, and I am sure she could learn more if someone had the time to work with her," he added. Mario had always wanted to have a dog, but with all his sports and camping activities, he didn't have time to care for one.

Lionel smiled. "It's hard to see how anything good could come from getting lost and needing a new home," he said. "Only a person with extra time on his hands. . ."

". . . who can't play baseball or swim or go to camp would have time to care for this dog!" finished Mario. "I could teach this dog lots of tricks, too. Mr. Nathan, this dog needs something good to happen for her, and I am hoping for something good to come from the change in my summer plans," cried Mario as he waved his cast for Mr. Nathan to see. "I'll take her!"

Mario knelt down to greet the dog. The eager puppy was happy to meet her new friend. She licked his hands and his cheek. "Don't you think you should check with your mom and dad, first?" asked Mr. Nathan.

"Nah," said Mario. "I'll just remind them of the family motto: expect something good to happen! They're going to love our new friend."

Lionel rolled his eyes. He knew his parents weren't going to be happy with Mario's discovery, but how could Lionel argue with the family motto?

73

Step 2 — Student Tips

To explain the author's purpose for writing, you need to remember:

- Tell why. "Why" is the reason the author wrote the text.

- Tell how. Find words or pictures that help you figure out the author's process for writing.

- Look for clues that tell you why authors write:

  Enjoyment (Funny sentences, interesting words, and images)

  Understand (Words that tell you what people (characters) are like and what they think, feel, or do)

  Find Out/Learn (Facts, charts, graphs, and pictures)

  Solve Problems (Words that tell you about an action or a decision)

  Persuade (Words that tell you how you should think)

Step 3

Complete the reading map. Use the reading map to help you think about the author's purpose.

Map 11a   Explain How and Why an Author Uses Contents of a Text to Support His/Her Purpose for Writing

I tell the process (how) and the reason (why) the story was written.

Purpose of Fiction	Purpose of Poetry	Purpose of Nonfiction
• enjoyment and entertainment • understand life, people, and experiences • find out about the lives of the characters and how they are similar to you • understand how characters solve problems that may be similar to yours	• enjoyment of the poet's feelings • expressive words and images • understand the poet's thoughts about life • find out about the subject • solve problems in your life by comparing them to the poet's writing	• enjoyment • understand something • give information, facts, or data • help you solve problems • figure out how to do something • persuade you to agree with the author

Circle the type of writing.	Tell why the story was written by writing the author's purpose for the story. (Pick an answer from the purpose boxes.)
fiction poetry nonfiction	

Write sentences from the text that show how the author tells the purpose for writing.
_____ _____ _____

Step 4 — **Read the following questions and write your answers.**

1. What is the type of writing in this story?

_____

_____

_____

2. How did you figure out the purpose of the story?

_____

_____

_____

3. Why was the story written? Explain how you figured out the answer.

_____

_____

_____

4. Is the story successful in achieving its purpose? Give a reason for your answer.

_____

_____

_____

Activity 11b

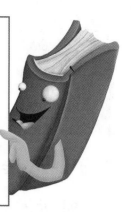

Explain How and Why an Author Uses Contents of a Text to Support His/Her Purpose for Writing

I tell the process (how) and the reason (why) the story was written.

Step 1

Read the announcement "Join the Bell Choir."

Join the Bell Choir

WHO IS INVITED?

You are invited to join the Cedartown Community Bell Choir. If you can count, you can play the bells. All ages are welcome.

WHAT WILL YOU DO?

After just a few practices, you will be ready to play with the bell choir. No experience necessary. We will teach you everything you need to know to be a bell ringer. And we supply the bells!

WHEN AND WHERE IS PRACTICE?

Our group practices every Tuesday afternoon from 3:00 p.m. to 4:00 p.m. at the community center located on Spruce Drive.

WHY SHOULD YOU JOIN?

Come and meet new friends and have fun. Free refreshments are served after practice. Please join us!

Step 2

Student Tips

To explain the author's purpose for writing, you need to remember:

- Tell why. "Why" is the reason the author wrote the text.

- Tell how. Find words or pictures that help you figure out the author's process for writing.

- Look for clues that tell you why authors write:

  Enjoyment (Funny sentences, interesting words, and images)

  Understand (Words that tell you what people (characters) are like and what they think, feel, or do)

  Find Out/Learn (Facts, charts, graphs, and pictures)

  Solve Problems (Words that tell you about an action or a decision)

  Persuade (Words that tell you how you should think)

Step 3

Complete the reading map. Use the reading map to help you think about the author's purpose.

Map 11b   Explain How and Why an Author Uses Contents of a Text to Support His/Her Purpose for Writing

I tell the process (how) and the reason (why) the story was written.

Purpose of Fiction	Purpose of Poetry	Purpose of Nonfiction
• enjoyment and entertainment • understand life, people, and experiences • find out about the lives of the characters and how they are similar to you • understand how characters solve problems that may be similar to yours	• enjoyment of the poet's feelings • expressive words and images • understand the poet's thoughts about life • find out about the subject • solve problems in your life by comparing them to the poet's writing	• enjoyment • understand something • give information, facts, or data • help you solve problems • figure out how to do something • persuade you to agree with the author

Circle the type of writing.	Tell why the story was written by writing the author's purpose for the story. (Pick an answer from the purpose boxes.)
fiction poetry nonfiction	

Write sentences from the text that show how the author tells the purpose for writing.

_____

_____

_____

Step 4

Read the following questions and write your answers.

1. What type of writing is the text?

_____

_____

_____

2. What is the reason the text was written?

_____

_____

_____

3. How did you figure out why the text was written?

_____

_____

_____

4. Write a sentence from the text that showed you how the author told his or her purpose for writing.

_____

_____

_____

Activity 12a

Identify Main Idea/Supporting Details

I figure out the overall idea and supporting details of the story.

Step 1

Read the text "Common Properties."

Common Properties

Scientists classify materials. They put materials like glass and metals into separate groups in order to study them more easily. Take glass, for example. Glass is hard. It can't bend. It's not magnetic.

Another group with properties is metal. Metals can be somewhat soft. They can be bent. Some metals are magnetic. Glass and metal are different in many properties. Classifying helps scientists understand materials better.

Step 2

Student Tips

To identify the main idea and supporting details, you need to remember:

- There is a main idea sentence in each paragraph. The main idea sentence tells what the paragraph is about.

- There are detail sentences in each paragraph. Detail sentences support the main idea, explain the main idea, and give information about the main idea.

Step 3

Complete the reading map. Use the reading map to help you think about the main idea and supporting details.

Map 12a　Identify Main Idea/Supporting Details

I figure out the overall idea and supporting details of the story.

Read each paragraph
to tell what the selection is about.

What is the main idea of paragraph 1?	What is the main idea of paragraph 2?
_____	_____
_____	_____
_____	_____
Details: Write words from the selection that support, explain, or give information about the main idea of paragraph 1.	**Details:** Write words from the selection that support, explain, or give information about the main idea of paragraph 2.
_____	_____
_____	_____
_____	_____
_____	_____

When I think about the main ideas of paragraphs 1 and 2, I decide the **overall** main idea of the selection is . . .

_____

_____

_____

Step 4   **Read the following questions and write your answers.**

1. What is the main idea of the first paragraph?

_____

_____

_____

2. What is one detail that tells you a property of glass?

_____

_____

3. Write an important detail from the second paragraph that tells you about metal.

_____

_____

4. What is the main idea of the second paragraph?

_____

_____

_____

5. In your own words, write the main idea of the whole selection.

_____

_____

Activity 12b

Identify Main Idea/Supporting Details

I figure out the overall idea and supporting details of the story.

Step 1

Read the story "A Pioneer School."

A Pioneer School

A long time ago, pioneer children went to schools much different from schools today. Most pioneer schools had only one room for children of all ages from the farming community. The school had a fireplace or a stove that the teacher had to keep filled up with logs or coal in order to keep the building warm on cold winter days. The floors and benches in the schools were made from wood, which was probably chopped from trees nearby.

Children had different experiences in the pioneer school than we do in schools today. Young and old children studied next to each other or in small groups. Children used small chalkboards and chalk to write their answers while sitting at their desks. Lunch was never made at school, so the children would bring lunches from home. Although the children learned the same basics of reading, writing, and math that are learned by children today, they learned them in a very different environment.

Step 2

Student Tips

To identify the main idea and supporting details, you need to remember:

• There is a main idea sentence in each paragraph. The main idea sentence tells what the paragraph is about.

• There are detail sentences in each paragraph. Detail sentences support the main idea, explain the main idea, and give information about the main idea.

Step 3

Complete the reading map. Use the reading map to help you think about the main idea and supporting details.

© 2005 Englefield & Associates, Inc.

Map 12b	Identify Main Idea/Supporting Details

I figure out the overall idea and supporting details of the story.

Read each paragraph
to tell what the selection is about.

What is the main idea of paragraph 1?	What is the main idea of paragraph 2?
_____	_____
_____	_____
_____	_____
Details: Write words from the selection that support, explain, or give information about the main idea of paragraph 1.	**Details:** Write words from the selection that support, explain, or give information about the main idea of paragraph 2.
_____	_____
_____	_____
_____	_____
_____	_____

When I think about the main ideas of paragraphs 1 and 2, I decide the **overall** main idea of the selection is . . .

_____

_____

_____

Step 4

Read the following questions and write your answers.

1. What is the main idea of the first paragraph?

_____

_____

_____

2. Write one sentence from the first paragraph that gives information about the main idea.

_____

_____

_____

3. What is the main idea of the second paragraph?

_____

_____

_____

4. Write one sentence that supports the main idea of the second paragraph.

_____

_____

_____

Activity 13a

Respond to the Text
I tell my thoughts, feelings, or observations of something similar to what happens in the story.

Step 1

Read the story "The Birthday Surprise."

The Birthday Surprise

"Today is going to be a great day," thought Olivia. It was her birthday. Olivia quickly got out of bed and hurried downstairs for breakfast. She knew today was her special day, and someone would certainly say, "Happy Birthday." They always celebrated her birthday with hugs, presents, cake, and a birthday song. That did not happen on this day. No one in her family said anything about her birthday. Olivia thought they had forgotten. She felt disappointed. She finished her breakfast and walked to school.

On the way to school, Olivia saw her friends, Lu and Debbie. They talked about the skating show they saw at the park last night. They also talked about their homework. Lu and Debbie didn't say, "Happy Birthday," to Olivia either. This was the first time her friends had not remembered her birthday. "We always do things together on my birthday, so they must have forgotten," thought Olivia. Olivia was puzzled when her friends did not say anything about her birthday.

When Olivia got to school, she talked to lots of people in her class. She talked about a lot of things. Olivia was thinking everyone must have forgotten her birthday. There was even a birthday chart on the wall. For the rest of the day, Olivia was hoping someone would remember her birthday. She did not want to be rude by reminding her friends they had forgotten her special day.

Olivia walked home slowly by herself. She thought she might watch some TV or read a book to forget about how bad she felt. This was the first time no one even said, "Happy Birthday," to her on her birthday.

When she got home, Olivia walked through the house. It was so quiet. She sadly went to the living room, then to the dining room looking for her mom. No one seemed to be home. As Olivia walked into the kitchen, she heard a loud, "Surprise!" The room was full of her friends and family. There were balloons, a cake, and presents. Best of all, everyone sang, "Happy Birthday." She was so happy to have this surprise party! Everyone was laughing about how they had pretended to forget her birthday. After the party was over, Olivia thought about how wonderful her friends and family were to plan such a special surprise party.

Step 2

Student Tips

To respond to the text, you need to remember:

• Tell your thoughts, feelings, and things you do or see that are like things in the story. Does the character think or feel like you do? Does the character act or talk like you? Does the setting make you think about something that has happened to you?

• Look for feeling words to describe emotions. Some emotion words like happy, sad, and afraid are on the reading map. Use these words to tell how you feel about the story.

Step 3

Complete the reading map. Use the reading map to help you think about the story.

Map 13a

Respond to the Text
I tell my thoughts, feelings, experiences, or observations
of something similar to what happens in the story.

After reading the story, tell your thoughts and feelings of something
similar that happened to you. Use your own feeling words or use the
bank below to help you.

_____

_____

_____

After reading the story, tell about experiences or observations you have
had of a similar thing.

_____

_____

_____

Bank of words to describe how you might feel

Happy	Angry	Afraid	Depressed
Glad	Enraged	Frightened	Down
Pleased	Furious	Scared	Rotten
Proud	Mad	Shaky	Sad
Wonderful	Upset	Worried	Tearful

Step 4

Read the following questions and write your answers.

1. What happened in the story that was different from what Olivia expected?

_____

_____

_____

2. How would you feel if your friends surprised you with a birthday party? Why would you feel this way?

_____

_____

_____

3. Why didn't Olivia remind anyone that it was her birthday? What would you have done?

_____

_____

_____

4. Tell about a time you or someone you know was surprised by something that happened.

_____

_____

Activity 13b

Respond to the Text

I tell my thoughts, feelings, or observations of something similar to what happens in the story.

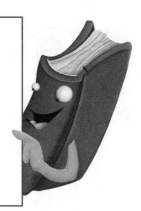

Step 1

Read the story "Shadow."

Shadow

Shadow is a two-year-old black Labrador retriever. She is a friendly dog who lives with a man named Jason. Shadow's best friends are Happy Cat and Herbie, a baby basset hound. Shadow enjoys running and playing with her friends. Most of all, she loves to travel with Jason.

Every morning, Shadow watches Jason get ready for his day. On the weekends, Jason takes Shadow and her friends, Herbie and Happy Cat, different places. They all hop into the truck, look out the window, and enjoy the ride.

One day, Shadow noticed that Jason had his camping gear packed. Jason looked worried and a little grumpy as he looked at the huge pile of camping gear in his truck. The truck was so full of camping gear, there was no room for Shadow and her friends. Shadow asked Happy Cat and Herbie to think of ways to solve the problem. Shadow knew she could not fit in the truck with all the camping gear. Happy Cat and Herbie were sad because they knew Shadow loved to go on trips. Shadow tried to stay calm and tried not to worry about missing the camping trip, but she was wondering who would take care of her while Jason was gone.

As the trip got closer, the pile of camping gear grew and grew. Jason seemed so excited. Shadow tried not to worry about missing the fun. Happy Cat and Herbie tried to comfort her. Shadow was wishing she could be included in the trip.

The next day, Shadow noticed a large box on the top of the truck. Shadow's friends came over and watched Jason put all the gear inside of the box. He looked very happy now that he had solved the problem of where to put all the camping gear. Shadow also saw her favorite toys placed inside the truck. She knew there would now be room for her inside of the truck. Shadow felt so happy, she started to jump for joy.

Just then, Jason called Shadow to the truck. Happy Cat and Herbie were invited also. Everyone jumped in the truck. Away they went to the campsite. Shadow felt like the luckiest dog in the world. She knew Jason made an extra effort so she and her friends could take the trip together.

Step 2

Student Tips

To respond to the text, you need to remember:

- Tell your thoughts, feelings, and things you do or see that are like things in the story. Does the character think or feel like you do? Does the character act or talk like you? Does the setting make you think about something that has happened to you?

- Look for feeling words to describe emotions. Some emotion words like happy, sad, and afraid are on the reading map. Use these words to tell how you feel about the story.

Step 3

Complete the reading map. Use the reading map to help you think about the story.

Map 13b	**Respond to the Text** I tell my thoughts, feelings, experiences, or observations of something similar to what happens in the story.

After reading the story, tell your thoughts and feelings of something similar that happened to you. Use your own feeling words or use the bank below to help you.

_____

_____

_____

After reading the story, tell about experiences or observations you have had of a similar thing.

_____

_____

_____

Bank of words to describe how you might feel

Happy	Angry	Afraid	Depressed
Glad	Enraged	Frightened	Down
Pleased	Furious	Scared	Rotten
Proud	Mad	Shaky	Sad
Wonderful	Upset	Worried	Tearful

Step 4

Read the following questions and write your answers.

1. As Jason packed for the trip, how did Shadow feel? Write how you would feel if you were not able to go on a trip.

_____

_____

_____

2. Shadow enjoys running and playing with her friends. Write about two things you enjoy doing with your friends.

_____

_____

_____

3. How did Shadow feel when she knew her friends would be able to go on the trip with her? How would you feel if you could take your friends on a trip?

_____

_____

_____

4. Shadow knew Jason went to extra trouble to include her and her friends on the trip. Tell about your observation or experience of including someone.

_____

_____

_____

Activity 14a

Evaluate and Critique the Text
I tell about the strengths and the weaknesses of what I read.

Step 1

Read the article "Electricity."

Electricity

Go turn on your radio, your TV, or your light. Guess what? You have started a parade. Yes, that's right, a parade of small electrons, pushing, bumping, and marching along. Did you know electricity is made of moving electrons? The energy of the moving electrons is called electricity. It is this energy that makes your radio, TV, or light turn on. You cannot feel the energy or see what it looks like. It makes no sound and has no color. However, you can see how electricity is used.

Here are several ways electricity is used.

In communication, electricity is used to power radios and televisions. Satellites circling Earth use electricity. Electricity powers our copy machines, fax machines, computers, and the equipment that prints our newspapers.

In our homes, we use electricity to wash our dishes and our clothes. We cook with ovens, microwaves, and toasters. Cooking is so much easier when we use electricity. Refrigerators and freezers cool our food and keep it from spoiling. Electric-powered heaters keep us warm in the winter, and air conditioners keep us cool in the summer, maintaining comfortable temperatures for us to live in.

In transportation, we use electricity to move people around all over the world. Elevators, subway cars, electric trains, and ships all use electricity to carry people to and from place to place. Traffic lights turn red, yellow, and green because of electricity.

Most people think we are lucky to have electricity, but some people think we should not use so much of it. By using electricity, we change how we live our lives. We no longer have to walk as much as people once did. We no longer have to build a fire to keep us warm at night. If we didn't have electricity, people would not have radio and television, and they would read more and talk with each other more. What do you think about how we use electricity?

The next time you turn on a button or switch, remember that inside a single wire, electrons are marching along. Lots of electrons go through the wires marching, pushing, and moving to help you live the way you do today.

Step 2

Student Tips

To evaluate and critique the text, you need to remember:

- List the strengths (good points) and weaknesses (bad points).

- See if the information agrees with the question. Ask yourself, "Does this information agree with the question? Does this information not agree with the question?"

- Tell why you think the answer is right.

Step 3

Complete the reading map. Use the reading map to help you think about how to evaluate and critique the text.

Map 14a

Evaluate and Critique the Text
I tell about the strengths and the
weaknesses of what I read.

Did the author convince you that electricity is a good thing?

The strengths are. . .

The weaknesses are. . .

After reading the strengths and weaknesses, the answer to the question is:

                   © 2005 Englefield & Associates, Inc.

Step 4

Read the following questions and write your answers.

1. Write one detail that supports using electricity for communication.

_____

_____

_____

2. How would we benefit from not using electricity?

_____

_____

_____

3. Do you think the author convinced you that the invention of electricity has helped people? Give a reason for your answer.

_____

_____

_____

4. Write one detail that tells how electricity has helped people in their homes.

_____

_____

_____

Activity 14b

Evaluate and Critique the Text

I tell about the strengths and the weaknesses of what I read.

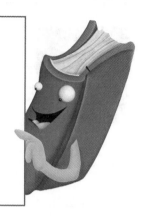

Read the story "Summer Job."

Summer Job

During the summer, Jose and Teresa earn money doing odd jobs and chores for people in their neighborhood. Jose likes to cut grass and to take care of pets while their owners are away. He cuts so much grass that his lawnmower blades become dull. He buys animal treats for the pets, which he takes to them when they have been inside all day.

Teresa likes to help paint fences and to baby-sit. She only has a big paintbrush, so sometimes it is difficult for her to paint in small places. She painted her neighbor's decorative garden fence, and her parents asked her to paint the fence around the rose bushes. She baby-sits every afternoon for three hours. When she baby-sits, she takes small toys, books, and treats to entertain the children.

When the end of the summer draws near, Jose and Teresa notice the sun setting earlier each day and the nights feeling cooler. They are so glad they had their summer jobs because they were able to save money to buy the things they want.

When Jose and Teresa decided to count their money, they had each earned more than two hundred dollars. Their parents said they each had to save half the money, but they could spend the other half on whatever they wanted.

The only thing Jose and Teresa do not like about working in the summer is they have less free time to do all the things they usually enjoy doing in the summer. They both wish they had more time to ride their bikes and play ball. However, after looking at all the money they earned, they both decided having summer jobs was a good way to spend their time.

Step 2

Student Tips

To evaluate and critique the text, you need to remember:

- List the strengths (good points) and weaknesses (bad points).

- See if the information agrees with the question. Ask yourself, "Does this information agree with the question? Does this information not agree with the question?"

- Tell why you think the answer is right.

Step 3

Complete the reading map. Use the reading map to help you think about how to evaluate and critique the text.

Map 14b

Evaluate and Critique the Text
I tell about the strengths and the
weaknesses of what I read.

**Did the author convince you that children
should have summer jobs?**

The strengths are. . .	The weaknesses are. . .
_____	_____
_____	_____
_____	_____
_____	_____
_____	_____
_____	_____
_____	_____

After reading the strengths and weaknesses, the answer to the question is:

_____

_____

_____

_____

Step 4   **Read the following questions and write your answers.**

1. Write one detail that **supports** children working in the summer.

_____

_____

_____

2. Do you think you would want to work in the summer? Why?

_____

_____

_____

3. Write one detail that **does not support** children working in the summer.

_____

_____

_____

4. Did the author convince you that children should have summer jobs? Explain your answer.

_____

_____

_____

Activity 15a

Summarize the Text
I tell the overall meaning of the text in my own words.

Step 1

Read the article "Levers: Simple Machines."

Levers: Simple Machines

Machines come in many shapes and sizes. When you think of a machine, you probably think of a large item, like a washing machine or a dishwasher. But machines can be small, too. Did you know that a pair of scissors is a machine? So are many other household items, such as can openers and screwdrivers. A machine is anything with fixed or moving parts that act together to do work. A machine is also something that changes the direction, the force, or the motion of something.

Levers are one type of machine. Levers are interesting machines because they make it possible to lift bigger things than you might normally be able to lift. If you go to the park, you might be able to find a lever machine to play on: a teeter-totter. How many times have you lifted your friends up high on a teeter-totter? You may have noticed you can even lift friends who are bigger than you. The reason you are able to lift them up so high is that you are using a machine called a lever.

Levers make pushing and pulling much easier, as well as making heavy things easier to lift. The part of the lever that decides how much you can lift is called the fulcrum. If you look closely at the teeter-totter, you will find a piece of wood or block under the middle of the board. That is the fulcrum, or the pivot point. Where you put the fulcrum will change the amount of weight you can lift with the lever. People have used lever machines, similar to teeter-totters, to move heavy things for centuries. Next time you are riding on a teeter-totter, remember that you really are using a machine!

Step 2

Student Tips

To summarize the text, you need to remember:

- Tell only the important information in each paragraph

- Leave out unimportant information

- Use you own words (different words that mean the same thing as the words in the story.)

- Make sure you stay on topic

Step 3

Complete the reading maps. Use the reading maps to help you think about your summary.

Map 15a.1

Summarize the Text
I tell the overall meaning of what I read
in my own words.

Summary Sentences
Cross out the unimportant information from paragraph 1.
Circle the most important details.

Machines come in many shapes and sizes. When you think of a machine, you probably think of a large item, like a washing machine or a dishwasher. But machines can be small, too. Did you know that a pair of scissors is a machine? So are many other household items, such as can openers and screwdrivers. A machine is anything with fixed or moving parts that act together to do work. A machine is also something that changes the direction, the force, or the motion of something.

Think about the most important information that you circled.
Now, use your own words to write one sentence that tells the
overall idea of the paragraph.

_____

_____

_____

_____

| **Map 15a.2** | Summarize the Text
I tell the overall meaning of what I read
in my own words. |

Summary Sentences
Cross out the unimportant information from paragraph 2.
Circle the most important details.

Levers are one type of machine. Levers are interesting machines because they make it possible to lift bigger things than you might normally be able to lift. If you go to the park, you might be able to find a lever machine to play on: a teeter-totter. How many times have you lifted your friends up high on a teeter-totter? You may have noticed you can even lift friends who are bigger than you. The reason you are able to lift them up so high is that you are using a machine called a lever.

Think about the most important information that you circled. Now, use your own words to write one sentence that tells the overall idea of the paragraph.

_____

_____

_____

_____

Map 15a.3

Summarize the Text
I tell the overall meaning of what I read
in my own words.

Summary Sentences
Cross out the unimportant information from paragraph 3.
Circle the most important details.

Levers make pushing and pulling much easier, as well as making heavy things easier to lift. The part of the lever that decides how much you can lift is called the fulcrum. If you look closely at the teeter-totter, you will find a piece of wood or block under the middle of the board. That is the fulcrum, or the pivot point. Where you put the fulcrum will change the amount of weight you can lift with the lever. People have used lever machines, similar to teeter-totters, to move heavy things for centuries. Next time you are riding on a teeter-totter, remember that you really are using a machine!

**Think about the most important information that you circled.
Now, use your own words to write one sentence that tells the
overall idea of the paragraph.**

_____

_____

_____

_____

Map 15a.4

Summarize the Text

I tell the overall meaning of what I read
in my own words.

Use your own words to write one sentence that tells the overall idea of the entire text.

Step 4

Read the following questions and write your answers.

1. Write two details from paragraph one that describe a machine.

_____

_____

_____

2. Write one sentence that summarizes the description of a lever.

_____

_____

_____

3. Write the important details that tell you how levers are used.

_____

_____

_____

4. Write a sentence that summarizes the text.

_____

_____

_____

Activity 15b

Summarize the Text

I tell the overall meaning of the text in my own words.

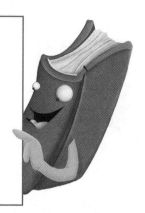

Step 1

Read the poem "Betty the Bird."

cheer, cheer, cheerful, cheer

Betty the Bird

Betty the bird is the prettiest in town.
She likes to fly high and flutter around.
She flies up to the trees way up in the sky,
And sits in the trees with her head held up high.

Betty the bird has a soft, lilting voice;
Singing sweet songs is her favorite choice.
By day she sings out in a fun sing-along;
At night, she has dreams of singing her songs.

So don't be surprised if one day coming soon,
You hear Betty up in the trees, singing a tune.
And when you're outside, look for that pretty bird,
Singing the sweetest sounds you've ever heard.

Step 2

Student Tips

To summarize the text, you need to remember:

- Tell only the important information in each paragraph

- Leave out unimportant information

- Use you own words (different words that mean the same thing as the words in the story.)

- Make sure you stay on topic

Step 3

Complete the reading maps. Use the reading maps to help you think about your summary.

Map 15b.1

Summarize the Text
I tell the overall meaning of what I read
in my own words.

Summary Sentences
**Cross out the unimportant information from stanza 1.
Circle the most important details.**

Betty the bird is the prettiest in town.
She likes to fly high and flutter around.
She flies up to the trees way up in the sky,
And sits in the trees with her head held up high.

**Think about the most important information that you circled.
Now, use your own words to write one sentence that tells the
overall idea of the paragraph.**

_____

_____

_____

_____

Map 15b.2

Summarize the Text

*I tell the overall meaning of what I read
in my own words.*

Summary Sentences
**Cross out the unimportant information from stanza 2.
Circle the most important details.**

Betty the bird has a soft, lilting voice;
Singing sweet songs is her favorite choice.
By day she sings out in a fun sing-along;
At night, she has dreams of singing her songs.

**Think about the most important information that you circled.
Now, use your own words to write one sentence that tells the
overall idea of the paragraph.**

_____

_____

_____

_____

Map 15b.3

Summarize the Text
I tell the overall meaning of what I read
in my own words.

Summary Sentences
**Cross out the unimportant information from stanza 3.
Circle the most important details.**

So don't be surprised if one day coming soon,
You hear Betty up in the trees, singing a tune.
And when you're outside, look for that pretty bird,
Singing the sweetest sounds you've ever heard.

**Think about the most important information that you circled.
Now, use your own words to write one sentence that tells the
overall idea of the paragraph.**

_____

_____

_____

_____

Map 15b.4

Summarize the Text
I tell the overall meaning of what I read
in my own words.

Use your own words to write one sentence that tells the overall idea of the entire text.

Step 4

Read the following questions and write your answers.

1. What important detail from the first stanza in the poem tells you what Betty the Bird likes to do?

   _____

   _____

   _____

2. What important detail from the second stanza tells you what Betty the Bird enjoys doing?

   _____

   _____

   _____

3. Write a detail that tells how Betty sounds when she sings.

   _____

   _____

   _____

4. Write one sentence that summarizes what you may hear if you find Betty the Bird outside.

   _____

   _____

   _____

Activity 16a

Identify Cause and Effect

I read to find out the reason why something happened and what happened.

Step 1

Read the article "Sailing with a Compass."

Sailing with a Compass

Can you imagine being out on a boat in the middle of the ocean? All you would see is endless water below you and endless sky above. How would you know what direction to sail? How would you find your way home? How would you know if you were continuing to sail in one direction and not just going around in circles? That's how it was for the world's first sea adventurers until they learned how to use the sky to help them find their way.

Early sailors knew certain things about the sky. They used the sun, the stars, and the moon to guide them to where they wanted to go. By paying close attention and charting these things, they learned how to stay on course and not to get lost. As a result, sailors could tell what direction they were going. It took a lot of knowledge and practice to become good navigators, but over time, the sailors mastered this skill and could find their way almost anywhere.

Later, a tool called a compass was developed. Sailors put a magnet on a piece of cork to make a compass. The magnetized metal always pointed north. Knowing that the compass magnet always pointed toward the north, sailors learned to set courses by devising a system that divided the world up into parts called degrees. They could set a course based on how many degrees away from north they wanted to go. Compasses were more accurate in finding directions than the sky, so sailors got lost even less than before. Even today, with all kinds of high tech equipment, sailors continue to use compasses to find their way across the ocean.

Step 2 — Student Tips

To identify cause and effect, you need to remember:

- The **cause** is the action or the reason that makes something happen (why something happened).

- The **effect** is the result (what happened).

- Look for key words that are clues to help you figure out if the statement is a cause or an effect.

  - Some of the key words that tell you why something happened (cause) are: **because**, **since**.

  - Some of the key words that tell you what happened (effect) are: **therefore**, **as a result**.

<u>Example Sentences</u>

Here is an example of a cause and effect sentence:

- **Because** gold was discovered in the west (cause), many people moved to the west to get wealthy (effect).

Sometimes the order is reversed and the effect comes before the cause. Here is an example of an effect and cause sentence:

- Many people moved to the west (effect) **because** gold was discovered (cause).

Step 3 — Complete the reading map. Use the reading map to help you think about cause and effect.

Map 16a

Cause and Effect
I read to find out the reason why something
happened and what happened.

They used the sun, stars, and moon to guide them.

Because →

Cause: **Why** something
happened
(Reason/Action)

Effect: **What** happened
(result)

Today, sailors can find the direction they want to go.

As a result →

Effect: **What** happened
(result)

Cause: **Why** something
happened
(Reason/Action)

Step 4

Read the following questions and write your answers.

1. What was the result of early sailors using the sun, the stars, and the moon to guide them?

_____

_____

_____

2. Why are sailors today able to find the direction they want to go?

_____

_____

_____

3. What were the results of sailors learning that magnetized metal always pointed north?

_____

_____

_____

4. What is the reason sailors divided the Earth into degrees?

_____

_____

_____

Activity 16b

Identify Cause and Effect

I read to find out the reason why something happened and what happened.

Step 1

Read the article "How Cars Changed Our World."

How Cars Changed Our World

Have you ever wondered how many things in our world have changed because of the invention of the car? Just take a ride down the street to see for yourself all the things that would be different if we did not have cars today. How many things can you think of that the invention of cars has changed in the world?

Although paved roads were developed well before cars were invented, they were not as common or as necessary as they are today. Early roads were sometimes paved with stones, logs, boards, or brick, but most roads remained dirt roads. The problem with dirt roads was they became very muddy when it rained. In earlier times, horses could easily travel on the muddy roadways, but the wheels of wagons and carriages often became stuck in the messy mud. As cars became more popular after World War I, people soon realized that the dirt roads that covered most of the country needed better surfaces. This was because the weight of the cars made it much more difficult for them to travel through muddy areas. Construction workers and engineers used asphalt, which created a hard, smooth surface, to pave many of the dirt roads. Soon, the number of paved roads began to grow, linking major cities together and making travel across the country easier. Today, there are many roads winding throughout the country, most of which are paved with asphalt. In fact, it is a rare sight to see a road that is not paved with anything.

Because roadways were becoming easier to travel on, people were able to get around more quickly than before. They were also able to travel more often. Before the invention of cars, it was not uncommon for people to stay very close to their homes for most of their lives. That changed when cars and improved roadways made travel simpler and quicker than before. It was common for people to go on Sunday drives where they would get to see places in the nearby countryside they had never seen before. The beautiful open spaces appealed to many people who lived in the city.

When cars became affordable for the average family, many people no longer had to live in the city to be close to where they worked. They realized they could move farther out of the crowded city and buy larger pieces of land at less expensive prices than in the city. Small towns near the bigger cities became residential communities, and the land in between was populated with people looking for their own pieces of land. Eventually, these communities came to be known as suburbs. People began to desert the cities, and shopping areas were built around the new areas where people lived. Even though the populations of cities were declining, the larger area of suburbs around the cities was growing, increasing the greater metropolitan areas.

The next time you are out riding in an automobile, look around you and imagine what the world would be like if there were no cars. You will be surprised at what you can come up with.

Step 2

Student Tips

To identify cause and effect, you need to remember:

- The **cause** is the action or the reason that makes something happen (why something happened).

- The **effect** is the result (what happened).

- Look for key words that are clues to help you figure out if the statement is a cause or an effect.

  - Some of the key words that tell you why something happened (cause) are: **because**, **since**.

  - Some of the key words that tell you what happened (effect) are: **therefore**, **as a result**.

Example Sentences

Here is an example of a cause and effect sentence:

- **Because** gold was discovered in the west (cause), many people moved to the west to get wealthy (effect).

Sometimes the order is reversed and the effect comes before the cause. Here is an example of an effect and cause sentence:

- Many people moved to the west (effect) **because** gold was discovered (cause).

Step 3

Complete the reading map. Use the reading map to help you think about cause and effect.

　　　　COPYING IS PROHIBITED　　　　© 2005 Englefield & Associates, Inc.

Map 16b

Cause and Effect
I read to find out the reason why something happened and what happened.

Effect: **What** happened (result)

Cars were invented.

As a result

Cause: **Why** something
happened
(Reason/Action)

Effect: **What** happened (result)

Step 4

Read the following questions and write your answers.

1. What is one result that happened because cars were invented?

_____

_____

_____

2. Write a second result that happened because cars were invented.

_____

_____

_____

3. Why did cars need paved roads more than horses and buggies did?

_____

_____

_____

4. Why did the populations of cities begin to decline?

_____

_____

_____

Activity 16c

Identify Cause and Effect

I read to find out the reason why something happened and what happened.

Step 1

Read the article "The United States Becomes a Nation."

The United States Becomes a Nation

The United States has not always been the land of the free and the home of the brave. In fact, the United States has not always been the United States. Before the United States became a nation, it was a group of colonies ruled by the government and king in England. How did this country go from being a bunch of colonies to an independent nation?

At first, the colonists enjoyed a pleasant relationship with England. England allowed its people to travel to the colonies in order to promote the growth of the English empire. Colonists were expected to remain loyal to England, to pay taxes to the English government, and to supply England with resources found in the colonies. These resources included things such as lumber, tobacco, and other raw materials. The English would use these materials to make items to be sold at market in both Europe and the colonies.

At first, this relationship worked well for both the colonies and England. As the number of colonists grew, though, some colonists thought England was taking advantage of the colonies. In places like Virginia and Pennsylvania, people met to discuss the creation of an independent country. This new country would have its own laws and its own government and would be free from English rule.

A group of representatives from each of the 13 English colonies met to discuss the idea of independence. They decided to write down the reasons why they thought the colonies deserved to be free from England. This list of reasons was put into a document called the Declaration of Independence. Some of the reasons they listed talked about how they thought they were treated unfairly by the King of England and the English government. Other reasons talked about how they thought they deserved new freedoms. These freedoms are part of the American way today, but colonists did not have many rights or freedoms.

The colonists signed this declaration and sent it to the King of England himself. The English did not want to lose their colonies and did not think the colonists deserved the rights and the freedoms they wanted. The King of England sent soldiers to the colonies to prevent the colonists from gaining independence. A war began between the colonists and the English soldiers. This was the Revolutionary War. After a few years of fighting, the colonists won the war, and the English were forced to leave the colonies. The colonies soon united into a new nation which we know as The United States of America.

Step 2

Student Tips

To identify cause and effect, you need to remember:

- The **cause** is the action or the reason that makes something happen (why something happened).

- The **effect** is the result (what happened).

- Look for key words that are clues to help you figure out if the statement is a cause or an effect.

  - Some of the key words that tell you why something happened (cause) are: **because**, **since**.

  - Some of the key words that tell you what happened (effect) are: **therefore**, **as a result**.

Example Sentences

Here is an example of a cause and effect sentence:

- **Because** gold was discovered in the west (cause), many people moved to the west to get wealthy (effect).

Sometimes the order is reversed and the effect comes before the cause. Here is an example of an effect and cause sentence:

- Many people moved to the west (effect) **because** gold was discovered (cause).

Step 3

Complete the reading map. Use the reading map to help you think about cause and effect.

Cause and Effect
I read to find out the reason why something
happened and what happened.

Cause: Why something
happened
(Reason/Action)

Because

The colonists formed a new nation.

Effect: **What** happened (result)

Cause: Why something
happened
(Reason/Action)

Step 4

Read the following questions and write your answers.

1. Write one reason from the text that tells you why a new nation was created.

_____

_____

_____

2. Write another reason from the text that tells you why a new nation was created.

_____

_____

_____

3. Why was it necessary for the colonists to fight the English?

_____

_____

_____

4. Why did the colonists want a new government?

_____

_____

_____

Self-Scoring Chart

Rate how well you understand the critical-thinking steps by putting a star (★) for mastery, a plus sign (+) for making progress, and a minus sign (–) for needs help. You can rate what you know four different times.

Characters	1	2	3	4
Name a character				
Match sentences with the descriptions of the character				
Tell how the character impacts the story				
Tell how the story would be different if you changed a characteristic of the character				

Setting	1	2	3	4
Describe the setting: Tell where the story takes place				
Describe the setting: Tell when the story takes place				
Describe the setting: Tell what the setting looks like				
Tell how the setting affects the story				
Tell how the setting affects the events				
Change the setting: Change where the story takes place				
Change the setting: Change when the story takes place				
Change the setting: Change what the setting looks like				
Tell how the characters would be different if the setting changed				
Tell how the events would be different if the setting changed				

Plot	1	2	3	4
Describe the chain of events by writing the major events in correct order				
Change the plot by choosing an event to happen earlier or later				
Tell how the story is different when one of the events has been changed				
Take an event out of the story				
Tell what would be different if one of the events is left out of the story				
Write what would happen if the character's actions were different				

Problem/Solution	1	2	3	4
Know the definition of a problem and a solution				
Write the problem of the story you read				
Write the events that lead up to the solution				
Write the solution of the story				
Write a different problem by making up your own problem				
Write how the events would be different				
Write how the solution would be different				

Point of View	1	2	3	4
Know the definition and key word pronouns of each point of view				
Identify the point of view in the story				
Write sentences from the story that helped you figure out the point of view				
Tell why the author writes from the point of view				
Tell how changing the point of view would affect the story				

Theme	1	2	3	4
Name some ideas from the text that tell what the story is about				
Write the lessons that the character learned				
Write a sentence telling what the message of the story is				

Infer	1	2	3	4
Read each sentence and paragraph to find clues about the story's meaning				
Write a clue in the clue box				
Write about an experience or knowledge you have of a similar thing				
Put the clue and your experience or knowledge together to make an inference about what is happening in the story				
Read more of the story to see if the inference is correct				

	1	2	3	4
Predict				
Read each sentence and paragraph to find clues about the story's meaning				
Write a clue in the clue box				
Write about an experience or knowledge you have of a similar thing				
Put the clue and your experience or knowledge together to make a prediction about what will happen next				
Read more of the story to see if the prediction is correct				

	1	2	3	4
Compare and Contrast				
Write the names of the things to be compared and contrasted				
Describe the characteristics				
If the items have same characteristics, mark them with a plus sign (+)				
If the items have different characteristics, mark them with a minus sign (–)				

	1	2	3	4
Fact and Opinion				
Write sentences that tell you if the text is a fact or an opinion				
Write how the information can be proven by evidence or observation				
Write where you would look up information to check it				
Tell if the information is true for everyone				
Write key words that are clues to tell how someone thinks or feels				
Write how the information tells a personal belief or judgment				
Tell if the information is true for some people				

	1	2	3	4
Explain Purpose for Writing				
Know the definitions and purposes of fiction, poetry, and nonfiction				
Identify the type of writing				
Write the author's purpose				
Write a sentence or sentences from the story that show an example of the author's purpose				

	1	2	3	4
Main Idea/Supporting Details				
Know the definitions of main idea and of supporting sentences				
Write the general topic of a paragraph				
Write one sentence that tells the main idea (overall message about the topic)				
Write detail sentences (to support, explain, or give information)				

	1	2	3	4
Respond to the Text				
Read the text and write your thoughts and feelings of a similar thing				
Write about your experiences or observations of a similar thing				

	1	2	3	4
Evaluate the Text				
Read the question given by the teacher				
List the strengths of the text				
List the weaknesses of the text				
After reading the strengths and weaknesses, answer the question				

	1	2	3	4
Summarize the Text				
Write the important information from each paragraph				
Rewrite each paragraph using your own words				
Use your own words to tell the overall idea of the whole selection				

	1	2	3	4
Identify Cause and Effect				
Know the definitions of cause and effect				
Read the key words for cause and effect				
Write why something happened (the cause)				
Write what happened (the effect)				

Notes

Notes

Notes

Notes

COPYING IS PROHIBITED

Subject-Specific Skill Development
Workbooks Increase Testing Skills

Write on Target
for grades 1/2, 3, 4, 5, and 6
Includes Graphic Organizers

Read on Target
for grades 1/2, 3, 4, 5, and 6
Includes Reading Maps

Math on Target for grades 3, 4, and 5
Includes Thinking Maps

For more information, call our toll-free number: 1.877.PASSING (727.7464)
or visit our website: www.showwhatyouknowpublishing.com